DINNER *then* DESSERT

DINNER *then* DESSERT

Satisfying Meals Using Only **3**, **5**, or **7** Ingredients

SABRINA SNYDER

with Jenny Wapner

PHOTOGRAPHS BY COLIN PRICE

HARPER
DESIGN
An Imprint of HarperCollins Publishers

HarperCollins books may be purchased for educational, business,
or sales promotional use. For information please email the
Special Markets Department at SPsales@harpercollins.com.

First published in 2021 by Harper Design
An Imprint of HarperCollinsPublishers
195 Broadway
New York, NY 10007
Tel: (212) 207-7000
Fax: (855) 746-6023
harperdesign@harpercollins.com
www.hc.com

Distributed throughout the world by
HarperCollinsPublishers
195 Broadway
New York, NY 10007
ISBN 978-0-06-299541-4
Library of Congress Control Number: 2021005554
Printed in Malaysia
First Printing, 2021

Design by Rae Ann Spitzenberger
Photographs by Colin Price

For my family,
you're my
everything.

INTRODUCTION

My Approach to Cooking

Inspiration is great, but planning is more reliable. I'm a planner. And in my opinion, there's no better reflection of good planning in the kitchen than a smartly stocked pantry. I'm not talking about cans of chili or chicken noodle soup that you rediscover years later and need to dust off before using, but shelf-stable components that can easily be transformed (with just a few other ingredients) into a nutritious, filling, and economical meal. We all have days when it feels like the only two options for dinner are takeout or a bowl of cereal, but if you know how to stock your pantry, a home-cooked meal can actually be faster than delivery. My hope is that even when you're short on time, inspiration, or ingredients, these recipes, which rely heavily on pantry ingredients, will be your ticket to a satisfying meal.

About Me and *Dinner Then Dessert*

I come to this material honestly: I feed my husband and three kids three meals a day nearly 365 days a year. Before I started my website, *Dinner Then Dessert*, I worked for over a decade cooking for other people's families as a private chef. I understand that cooking every night is tricky—and consistently cooking delicious food even more so. Add in dietary restrictions, picky eaters, and a lack of time, and you can feel as if you've failed before you've even started. What I've come to realize is the secret is not about trying to reinvent the wheel every night. It's about taking foundational recipes that are tried-and-true and then layering in new and interesting flavor combinations. Starting with workhorse recipes like roast chicken and meatloaf, crowd-pleasers like cheesy baked pasta, and time-savers like

slow-cooker chili, I test and retest them until they're perfect, then I add fun twists like BBQ chicken to mac and cheese, or Indian curry to meatballs. The recipes in this book are practical and flexible. They're also flavor-packed and fun.

I started *Dinner Then Dessert* because my clients were always asking for my recipes and I liked the idea of creating a resource where they could all be housed in one place. Designing and perfecting new recipes is my passion—nothing quirky or idiosyncratic, just reliable and highly tested. I take my cues from America's Test Kitchen and Serious Eats's Food Lab; I'm systematic and scientific in my approach, and I make sure that the recipes I give my readers are easy to follow and make. Cooking alongside clients for so many years, I've seen just about every conceivable "food fail," some more surprising than others. I always try to put myself in the kitchen with my readers, thinking about where their questions might come up, where they might get stuck. And if one of these recipes becomes a favorite, you will inevitably tire of it—that's why I give so many variations. Now you have multiple ways to make adjustments to it, either because you might be missing an ingredient or just want to mix it up—ensuring that you keep it in regular rotation.

Growing up in California, I spent hours watching *Yan Can Cook* and Wolfgang Puck, scribbling down recipes, then racing into the kitchen to re-create Martin Yan's beef stir-fry or practicing Wolfgang's technique for julienning vegetables. I loved being able to make small tweaks to flavors or cooking times and see big changes in the end result.

When I worked as a private chef, I often had to make a different meal for each member of the family—each with their own dietary restrictions or food preferences. And I'd often be preparing these several hours ahead of dinnertime, so the food would need to keep and reheat well. I loved the challenge, but I now had my own family to think about. So, with young kids at home, I needed a job that could accommodate my schedule. *Dinner Then Dessert* was born.

How This Book Is Organized

At its core, this book is intended to inspire and teach people to stock and cook from their pantry. I've devoted Part I of the book to listing and describing the ingredients that I turn to most often. I strongly believe that any item that takes up space on my pantry shelf should have multiple uses, so I try not to call for any ingredients that get used only once. Along with shelf-stable pantry items are perishable items—the meat and poultry, seafood, dairy, and fruits and vegetables that I use most often in my cooking. Among these are chicken thighs and breasts, larger cuts of meat that can be slow-cooked in advance, and bacon (which is a powerhouse in the kitchen for instant flavor). My hope is that working with a slightly pared-down assortment of ingredients will build your confidence. You will learn how each ingredient behaves in the kitchen, how long it needs to get tender and whether it can handle high heat, which flavors are complementary, and so on. From there you can make your own swaps and improvisations.

Part II of the book is broken down into three chapters on dinners (plus one on desserts), organized by the number of basic ingredients each recipe requires—3, 5, or 7. **These numbers don't include oil, butter, or salt and pepper.** Since shopping for a recipe is often the biggest roadblock to cooking, my hope is that these very simplified recipes remove that obstacle. If you have other herbs or vegetables that you want to throw in, by all means do it! But know that even without any extras, you can still make a delicious meal. Within each chapter, I've organized the recipes according to the most common and stress-free cooking methods: quick cooking on the stovetop, longer braising or using the slow-cooker, and baking. At the end of each section are easy side dishes that can be mixed and matched with other recipes in the book.

Sprinkled throughout the book are recipes that I consider foundational recipes. These are classics like roast chicken, pot roast, meatloaf, and roast pork loin. They are easy enough to make any night of the week but can also be dressed up and served to company. For these, I devote a bit more space to describing how to perfect your technique, and I give more ideas for additional seasonings and embellishments.

Finally, desserts, which are similarly organized by number of basic ingredients. I've included some of my favorite recipes here, ranging from brownies that can be decked out in a million different ways for the numerous bake sales you may have in your life to impressive mousses and pies destined for the holiday table.

How to Use This Book

While this book begins with a list of pantry staples, I certainly don't expect you to go out and buy everything on that list before getting started. Instead, I recommend studying your family's eating habits so you know how much you use various items. And then take a look at your pantry. Maybe there are things you buy that never seem to get used. What do you already have, what can you toss because it's been there for a decade? There is often a disconnect between how we would like to cook and eat and how we actually do, but it is not an impossible divide. Looking to incorporate more fruits and vegetables? Start with a few new additions. Or, if you're interested in incorporating more Asian or Latin American

flavors into your cooking, try a shelf-stable sauce or condiment or two; I've listed some of my favorites.

I grew up cutting coupons with my mother. While that now seems charmingly anachronistic, it taught me to look closely at what things cost and to learn how to comparison shop. It also revealed that there are cycles to pricing at grocery stores. Many items, like chocolate chips, butter, pasta sauce, and canned chicken broth will reliably go on sale, so it makes sense to organize your shopping to hit those sales. You don't need to mark your calendar, but you can buy a few more of those sale items so you're set until they go on sale again. And, relatedly, learn which ingredients to economize on—or not; sometimes a cheaper price means an inferior ingredient that will bring down the quality of the finished dish.

And for almost every recipe in the book, I've included a substitution chart. Don't have shrimp? Use chicken. Hate the taste of cumin? Use rosemary. The recipes are meant to be guides, not written law, and I hope the substitution charts will help you see how easily swaps can be made. The lack of a single ingredient shouldn't be an impediment—these are flexible recipes that can be adjusted and customized. Unless the substitution chart says otherwise, you can assume it is a direct substitution, using the ingredient in the same step of the directions as the ingredient it's replacing, with no change to the cook time unless otherwise noted. **Read down the chart for the substitutions in each variation.**

Part 1

PANTRY

BUILDING A PANTRY

While the word "pantry" conjures images of a cavernous room straight out of Downton Abbey, in our modern world a pantry can be as small as a single cupboard in your kitchen. For me, a smartly stocked pantry is central to efficient, economical cooking, and it's what makes it possible for me to create simple, satisfying meals throughout the week without needing to run out to the store for each meal. However, the operative phrase here is "smartly stocked." More can quickly become less when it comes to old, expired, or nonessential ingredients. Paring down your pantry makes it easier both to see what you have and to design meals around those ingredients. It reduces the likelihood that you'll overbuy, buy duplicates, or need to dump ingredients that have passed their prime. Just like a capsule wardrobe helps people see what they actually have in their closets and get dressed quickly, a right-sized pantry can free you up to think about dinner with fresh eyes. I like to think about my pantry and, in turn, my recipes, in terms of components: What are my proteins, my sweeteners, my salty elements? How can I mix it up to give chicken thighs an Asian-inspired twist one night and a Mexican flavor the next? The list that follows is a snapshot of the pantry items that I find to be essential, along with how to shop for and cook with them. When I refer to the "pantry," I'm including perishables in that list, though I've separated them from the shelf-stable items. These might be a backup pack of chicken thighs I throw in the freezer, or the bag of lemons that I make sure to always replenish. But first, here are a few rules of thumb that guide my food shopping.

I love the challenge of coming up with meals that are satisfying and delicious but require the fewest number of ingredients. The trick to cooking this way is to pay close attention to every item you purchase. And, because there is huge potential for savings in making recipes that only call for 3, 5, or 7 ingredients, it means you can spend a bit more and take more care with each ingredient. So, my **FIRST** rule of thumb is that quality matters.

We all love a bargain, and there are certainly places to economize when buying groceries (more about this on page 15), but when it comes to certain staples, don't get lured into buying an inferior product that will compromise the final dish. Honey, maple syrup, and balsamic vinegar are a few examples of ingredients where higher quality will make a difference. For proteins, especially when they're the centerpiece of the meal, it's important to seek out the best. For instance, I buy wild salmon, without any color added. It is more expensive than the farmed variety, but the difference in flavor, not to mention nutritional value, is significant. I know spending $20 at the grocery store for a pound of salmon can cause some sticker shock, but remember that your $20 purchase (along with just a few other ingredients) will create an impressive meal for two or three people.

The **SECOND** most important thing to keep in mind is shelf life. Many products can get forgotten in the back of a cupboard and kept beyond their recommended shelf life. Spices are a prime example of this. Keep an eye on those "best by" dates, since the longer dried spices sit on your shelf, the more they lose their potency.

THIRD, when maintaining a small pantry, buy only what you need. The desire to stock up seems to be an innately human urge, and one that is compounded by promotions and sale pricing, but buying two packages of bacon when you only need one means that most likely one of them is destined to die in the back of the fridge. Keep the stocking up to a reasonable amount, or those bargain ribs buried in the freezer will never see the light of day again.

FOURTH, be a smart shopper. While I'm not suggesting you order from a million online sites, or even drive around town to a dozen different markets, knowing which stores are best for different ingredients and augmenting your normal shopping with a few side trips every week or two can save you money as you seek out better ingredients. For instance, if my cooking one week will rely heavily on fresh produce, I'll head over to Sprouts, since they have the best prices in my area. Or, if I'll be grilling a lot of meat, I'll probably do more of my shopping at WinCo or Costco. In short, I don't rely on one store to meet all of my shopping needs. I also keep an eye on weekly ads to help determine which stores to go to that week. In addition to my regular shopping, I add a trip to an ethnic or specialty market about once a month to seek out unusual or hard-to-find ingredients. And, while I do keep an eye out for specials and promotions,

I don't drive across town chasing a sale on a single ingredient; that adds more stress (not to mention gas and time) than it's worth.

And finally, FIFTH, when buying meat, talk to the butcher! The meat counter can be a confusing place, but you can and should ask questions: Are those large chunks of short ribs or are they pieces that might have shards of bone in them? Do you have a chuck roast with more even marbling? Can I get a thicker cut of rib-eye? If you don't like what you see in the case, ask what else they have, or ask for a fresh cut. I find that questions like these can often turn into a friendly conversation about what I plan to do with that meat.

PERISHABLE PANTRY STAPLES

These are the proteins, dairy products, and fruits and vegetables that I use most often in my cooking and call for most frequently in the recipes in the book. The list below includes a little about why these are so important in the kitchen and what to look for when you're shopping for them.

Proteins

Beef

CHUCK ROAST

After chicken thighs, chuck roast, which is usually sold boneless, is the meat I turn to most often in my cooking. It's a cost-effective and easy cut to work with. Chuck takes to braising beautifully, and when it's cooked

Keeping Track of What's in Your Pantry

I'm sure I'm not alone in looking at my pantry and discovering half a dozen jars of barbecue sauce when the thing I actually need, canned tomatoes, is missing. Either my subconscious is telling me to barbecue more often, or it's just impossible to keep a mental shopping list. Back in my days as a private chef, I treated pantry inventory like the job it was and installed whiteboards in my clients' kitchens to keep track of what we were running low on; with these, I was able to get a sense of how quickly a family ran through items. After many years, I finally applied this same practice to my own kitchen (what's that expression—the shoemaker's children go barefoot?). For example, after tracking it, I now know that my family of five will use 2 pounds/1 kg of butter in one month. So if I see butter is on sale, I buy two boxes.

To keep a pantry inventory in your home, I recommend getting a spare notebook just for the kitchen. Write down the things you buy most frequently over the next couple of weeks. Then, as you use each item and discard the package, make a note of how long it took to go through it. After a couple of weeks, you'll have a pretty good idea of how fast you run through your staples and other basic ingredients.

Now that you have your handy checklist, you can plan your shopping trips to stores where those items are most competitively priced. With a well-tracked pantry, you'll find yourself making fewer unnecessary purchases, allowing you to keep your pantry smaller (even when stocking up!).

low and slow in your oven or slow cooker, a tough, marbled cut of meat is transformed into a tender, hearty meal for a crowd.

A couple of things to keep in mind when selecting chuck roast: first, make sure the roast has an even marbling of fat. The fat will break down as you cook the beef and create a tender roast. Second, be sure to buy a piece of meat that is of even thickness. For pot roast, I like it to be at least 2 inches/5 cm thick.

I am very particular about the meat I buy. I used to force my husband to send me photos from the supermarket to make sure he was getting the right cut. I typically avoid select cuts like blade roast or eye of round, which may have a similar shape to chuck roast and may be slightly cheaper, but they just don't compare.

The chuck roast (top) is an uneven cut with minimal marbling; the chuck roast (bottom) is what you want: a thick, even cut that is well marbled.

Chuck roast almost always calls for braising. For best results, start by salting the roast heavily and then browning it. For a 5- to 6-pound/2.25 to 2.7 kg chuck roast, I use about a tablespoon of kosher salt and a teaspoon of coarsely ground black pepper. To brown the meat, heat a few tablespoons of oil in a large Dutch oven, then carefully sear the roast for 5 to 7 minutes on each side. For more on browning meat, see page 147.

RIB EYE

There just isn't a more flavorful cut of steak than rib eye. A rib-eye steak has two sections, the eye, or loin, which is lean, and the cap (my personal favorite), which is fattier. Sometimes called the deckle or the spinalis, the cap is rich and buttery and tastes overwhelmingly extravagant.

When you're buying a rib-eye steak, talk to your butcher and make sure you aren't getting an end cut. End cuts usually don't have a thick cap, so they aren't as prized as a center cut. Also make sure to get a steak that is at least 1 inch/2.5 cm thick. I buy mine 2 inches/5 cm thick because the extra thickness keeps it moist as it cooks.

Because a rib-eye steak is so flavorful, the best way to serve it is with a very mild sauce that won't overwhelm it—or no sauce at all. When you have a prized ingredient like this one, focus your energy on getting the best version of it and cooking it to perfection.

FLANK STEAK

Flank steak is a popular cut valued for its low fat content and ease of cooking. Flank steak is best marinated and grilled or thinly sliced for stir-fries. Because it's so lean, it should be cooked quickly and at high heat to prevent it from becoming tough and dry. Equally important is cutting flank steak against the grain. Imagine the steak as a bundle of long thin ropes glued together. To serve it, you want to cut across those ropes, not parallel to them. This cuts each "rope" into little sections so that you don't end up with small bundles of fibers you have to chew through.

GROUND BEEF

Choosing ground beef can be confounding. There are many varieties each with different levels of leanness, depending on the percentage of meat to fat. These percentages range from 70/30 to 96/4. There's a way to use each, but most of the time, I opt for 85/15, which gives me enough fat to add flavor and moisture but not so much that I need to drain off fat after cooking. Ground beef that is 90/10 or higher is as lean as ground chicken. While this makes it healthier, it's often the case that you'll need to add some fat back in the form of oil later in your recipe. A quick note on home economics: The higher the fat content, the less expensive the beef will be, because meat is more desirable than fat. But much of the excess fat will render out during cooking, and you'll end up throwing it away. So, before you grab 70/30 ground beef because it costs less, remember that you'll actually end up with less meat.

Chicken and Turkey

CHICKEN THIGHS

I could write a book on my love for chicken thighs, but it all comes down to the cost, versatility, and flavor that make chicken thighs such a powerhouse ingredient. Many people reserve this cut for grilling or frying, but thighs are incredibly versatile. I buy bone-in, skin-on, thighs, which is the most affordable option. Bone-in, skin-on chicken thighs can do triple duty by providing meat, fat, and broth depending on how you use them. However, perhaps most important, is that chicken thighs are very easy to cook. Think of the fat and bones as an added layer of protection for the meat. Cooking chicken breasts can be unforgiving—if you cook them even a few minutes too long, you end up with dry meat—but thighs give you more room for error. The skin offers the meat additional moisture, and the bones provide added fat (and flavor) from within to keep the meat juicy. If you don't want to eat the skin, just remove it once you've finished cooking.

NOTE: *There is a lot of variation in the size of chicken thighs (and breasts). The recipes in this book usually call for 4 thighs to feed 4 people, but you may need to increase the number if your chicken thighs are on the small side.*

CHICKEN BREASTS

After my ode to chicken thighs, you might be expecting nothing but complaints about this leaner cut. But, if cooked correctly, chicken breasts are a delicious and valuable part of any kitchen arsenal. When cooking breasts, it's important to start with pieces of equal size and thickness. Packages of boneless, skinless breasts often contain different-sized pieces. Before cooking, trim the pieces so they are of roughly equal thickness.

Unlike thighs, which can handle slow cooking, like braising, chicken breasts shine when cooked quickly at high temperatures to preserve their flavor and keep them from drying out. When looking for swaps in this book, you'll notice I never swap in chicken breasts for chicken thighs in the braising and slow-cooking sections. Cooking chicken breasts low and slow will lead to dryness. Better to keep chicken breasts for quick stir-fries and sheet-pan meals.

MY FAVORITE CHICKEN-BREAST BAKING TIP: *Give your chicken breasts a quick sear in a hot skillet with a bit of oil to brown them before adding them to the other ingredients for a sheet-pan dinner. This jump start on browning will help keep them succulent.*

GROUND CHICKEN

Ground chicken is a great swap for ground beef when you're looking to make a dish healthier. This works best with thigh meat, though, as opposed to breast meat, because the thigh has a bit more fat. If you want to use ground breast meat, choose recipes that have another source of fat or moisture. For instance, I often use grated onions in kebabs (a nod to my Armenian heritage), which add both flavor and moisture. This is a great alternative to the milk-soaked bread called for in most meatball recipes. Ground chicken is best cooked quickly at high heat to prevent it from drying out.

GROUND TURKEY

Ground turkey is an easy substitute for ground chicken. I use regular ground turkey instead of ground turkey breast because it contains a small amount of fat, which adds needed moisture during cooking.

WHOLE CHICKEN

Many cooks think of whole chickens as just for roasting, but with a bit of creative thinking, you can turn this ingredient into a weeknight cooking staple.

Cutting the backbone out of a whole chicken and then pressing it flat, a technique called spatchcocking, will cut your roasting time in half. Want to make two easy meals in one? Buy a whole chicken and cut off the thighs and drumsticks. Then you can boil the chicken thighs and legs to make an easy base for chili and simmer the rest of the chicken for broth, reserving the cooked breast meat for salads or sandwiches. Sometimes I save excess chicken fat from the carcass for when I need a quick flavor boost in recipes that call for breast meat. If your chicken has extra flaps of skin, cut

these off with kitchen shears or a paring knife, arrange them in a single layer in a ziptop bag, and freeze. Frozen skin keeps for up to 3 months. Defrost it in the fridge before use, then render out the fat by cooking the skin in a pan over medium heat until it melts, discarding any remaining solids. I'll add a tablespoon or so of this fat when I'm cooking chicken breasts to help with even cooking and to add a bit more richness.

Pork

BACON

Bacon does triple duty in my kitchen: The meat itself is delicious, the rendered fat adds a nice smokiness to other dishes, and crisped bacon adds texture as a garnish. And you only need a little to add loads of flavor.

To give yourself the most flexibility in the recipes in this book, I recommend buying regular bacon, not thick cut or center cut. Thick-cut is great cooked and crumbled to use as a garnish, but it's hard to work with in recipes that call for wrapping slices of bacon around meat or vegetables.

When cooking bacon, I recommend underestimating the amount of time it needs. As it cools, it will become a bit crisper, and, if it's still limp, you can just reheat it for another 20 seconds or so in the pan. When cooked, it should be reddish, not brown.

GROUND PORK

Ground pork is an underused meat, but its neutral flavor means it's versatile enough to easily incorporate into your cooking.

With just a few spices, you can make your own breakfast patties. Or use it for meatloaf, meatballs, or even pork burgers. It's an affordable option and cooks quickly.

PORK LOIN

Pork loin is a large cut of lean meat covered with a thin fat cap. This flavorful cut lends itself well to roasting, and if it is placed fat side up in the pan, the fat will render during cooking and act as a natural baster for the meat.

When purchasing pork loin, buy only as much as you need, since, given its leanness, it doesn't reheat well and can become dry. I like to tie pork loin roasts with kitchen twine before cooking. This easy extra step ensures that the roast is of the same thickness throughout and will therefore cook evenly.

PORK SHOULDER

Pork shoulder, also known as pork butt or Boston butt, is the go-to choice for slow-cooker and long-braising recipes, guaranteeing moist, delicious, and juicy results even after being exposed to hours of heat. It's an inexpensive cut and, because of its high fat content, cooked pork shoulder freezes and reheats beautifully. You can find it with or without skin; I typically buy it without. Pork shoulder will release a lot of fat when cooking, most of which you'll want to drain off, so keep that in mind and add any sauce after cooking.

PORK SAUSAGE

Sausage is a flavor-packed protein that, like bacon, can carry a recipe almost by itself. I like to cut sausages into large pieces and then sear them, which preserves the texture but renders enough of the fat to flavor any vegetables that are cooking alongside them. If you find yourself with a lot of fat, store it in a jar in your fridge or freezer just as you would bacon fat. The flavor is deep and strong and can be a great addition to roasted vegetables, soups, or even roasts.

Sausage is naturally a high-fat protein. If you want to limit the amount of fat, you can use sausage as a flavor accent and supplement with a leaner meat like lean ground pork. This gives you a punch of flavor and allows you to control how much fat you keep in your recipe.

There are so many varieties of sausage, but I generally buy a mild pork sausage, like a sweet Italian, that won't overpower the flavors in the rest of the dish.

Seafood

SALMON

Salmon is a delicious and healthy protein as long as you're mindful about the salmon you buy. I only buy wild Alaskan salmon.

Although you can often find good deals at Costco and Whole Foods, it's always more expensive than farmed salmon, sometimes even twice the price. However, in my mind, this is money well spent. Wild salmon is naturally leaner and lower in toxins than the farmed variety; it's also full of omega-3s. And it gets its pink color naturally from the shrimp and krill the fish eat. Farmed salmon are kept in water pens and fed pellets containing corn, grains, and anchovies; their flesh is a dull gray and the farmers add artificial coloring to give it a reddish hue. In addition to better flavor, wild salmon is a more environmentally sustainable option.

SHRIMP

Shrimp always seem festive, and they have the potential to make as impressive a statement as lobster at a fraction of the price. And they cook in under five minutes, making them ideal for last-minute dinner parties.

Shrimp are sold according to the quantity per pound: for example, "13–15

How to Peel and Devein Shrimp

If you buy shrimp in the shell (they will be cheaper), always devein them. The dark line that runs along the top of the shrimp is the digestive tract, and you don't want to eat it. You can buy shrimp peeled and deveined, of course, but if you haven't, now is your chance to catch up on your favorite podcast. Grab a cutting board, a paring knife, and a couple of damp paper towels.

1 Pull away the shell of each shrimp just above the tail section.

2 Take a paring knife and make a shallow cut down the spine.

3 Using the paring knife or a fork, gently remove the black line that runs down the back of the shrimp; these are the intestines.

4 To remove the tails, squeeze just above the tail segment. You can also leave the tails on.

count shrimp" means there are 13 to 15 of this size per pound/455 g. This is the size I call for most often in the recipes in this book, and they are a great choice for stir-fries, shrimp and grits, and curries. If you're looking to make a big statement, big U–7 shrimp (indicating there are fewer than 7 shrimp per pound/455 g) are the way to go. Sometimes referred to as prawns, these are perfect for surf-and-turf spreads and delicious on the grill. A pound/455 g of these large shrimp will feed 2 or 3 people.

If buying frozen shrimp, look for peeled and deveined uncooked shrimp. Defrost the shrimp in cold water, drain in a colander, and pat dry with paper towels. Don't try to hurry your thawing process by using hot water, or you'll end up poaching the shrimp.

Shrimp are extremely quick cooking. If you're using them in soups or curries, add them just a few minutes before the end of cooking. If you're panfrying them or adding them to a stir-fry, make sure to dry them carefully or the moisture will cause the oil in the pan to splatter. And finally, never cook shrimp more than once; if you buy precooked shrimp, don't cook them again, or you'll end up with rubbery meat.

Dairy and Eggs

BUTTER

I always buy unsalted butter, because I like to be the one in control of how much salt is in my recipes. If you have salted butter, you can adjust your recipe accordingly: Salted butter contains about ¼ teaspoon salt per stick—not enough to make a noticeable difference in most savory recipes, but enough to make a sweet recipe taste just a little different. In cooking, butter adds a rich flavor, while vegetable oil adds no flavor. However, butter is not ideal for browning foods as it has a lower smoking point and will burn when exposed to high heat.

For baking recipes, I first freeze the butter and then chop it carefully into shards (like chopping a block of chocolate) or grate it with a box grater. Prepping the butter this way makes for really tender baked goods. You can store extra butter in the freezer (wrapped carefully in foil and then in an airtight plastic bag) for up to 4 months.

EGGS

My go-to are large cage-free eggs, either brown or white. Always keep eggs refrigerated except when you are using them for baking. In that case, take them out of the fridge one hour before needed. This is an important step, because eggs at room temperature will mix more evenly into batters and you'll also get better volume in your cake batters.

MILK

I grew up on 1% milk and continued to buy it out of habit into adulthood. It was what I used in my cooking simply because it was what I had on hand. But when my kids were born, I switched to whole milk for their sake and started using it in my cooking, without really thinking about it. That's when I discovered what I had been missing: Whole milk makes sauces significantly creamier and richer without adding a lot more fat or calories. I've actually cut back on heavy cream in some recipes because whole milk does the job so well.

All the recipes in this book were tested with whole milk, although you are, of course, free to use what you want. Just know that lower-fat milk will result in a sauce that may be a tad watery and less rich. On that note, I would not recommend swapping in fat-free milk unless you're reincorporating fat somewhere else in the recipe.

If you don't drink milk on a regular basis but you'd like to keep a small amount of dairy on hand for cooking, Trader Joe's sells shelf-stable whipping cream, which you can thin with a bit of water. I recommend this over rehydrated powdered milk.

I don't typically use heavy cream in my cooking (though it is essential in baking) because of the fat content (a whopping 36 percent milk fat)—and because a recipe will call for a small amount and the rest of the container will likely spoil in the fridge. However, heavy cream can be wonderful in some recipes. To simulate heavy cream, I'll make a roux from equal parts butter and flour, stirring them together in a saucepan, and then slowly whisk in whole milk to make a creamy white sauce that can be used with pasta or chicken.

PARMESAN CHEESE

Parmesan cheese adds flavor, fat, and salt to myriad dishes. You can buy a chunk of Parmesan to serve on a cheese board, or to add freshly shaved to pastas and other dishes. (Don't discard the rind—I add it to soups for a ton of extra flavor.) I find Trader Joe's to be a good spot to source high-quality Parmesan.

Buying grated Parmesan is a huge time saver. I use grated Parmesan as a component in breading since it helps crisp up whatever is being panfried. You can also buy shredded Parmesan to add as a topping for pasta, or shaved Parmesan, which adds a dramatic flair when added to finished dishes.

SOUR CREAM

Sour cream is a staple in our fridge, something we never go without. It is a low-cost, high-flavor, creamy addition to many recipes. It also happens to be one of the few ingredients where the low-fat version usually works just as well as the full-fat. Almost any soup or chili is immediately better with a quick spoonful. I think of sour cream as the dairy version of Better Than Bouillon (see page 35); it offers a punch of creaminess the same way BTB adds a punch of chicken or beef flavor.

Fruits and Vegetables

BELL PEPPERS

Green and red bell peppers are a mainstay in my kitchen. Red bell peppers are sweeter and more kid-friendly, and I also use them in any recipe that calls for uncooked peppers. Yellow or orange bell peppers can be used interchangeably with red ones. Green bell peppers have a bit of bitterness when raw, but they are a great complement to savory flavors like sausage, or alongside more herbaceous vegetables like fennel or celery. And they can offer a nice counterpoint to sweet sauces, as in stir-fries.

With any bell peppers, you should remove the stems and seeds. They aren't spicy like those of chili peppers, but they aren't edible either.

BROCCOLI

I buy broccoli crowns if they're on sale and whole bunches (stalks and crowns) when they are not. Make sure the florets are dark green and firm. Bendy or floppy stalks with yellowing florets indicate broccoli past its prime.

If you are buying whole bunches of broccoli, don't forget to use the stalks. When sliced thinly, about ¼ inch/6 mm thick, you can roast the stalks alongside your florets. Or, if peeled, the stalks can be steamed with the florets. If you are making a soup, simply dice the stalk and sauté alongside your mirepoix (chopped celery, carrots, and onion) for more flavor.

CARROTS

Carrots are inexpensive, versatile, and have an admirably long shelf life. I use them raw, steamed, or roasted (they're best and sweetest when roasted).

I buy carrots in 5-pound/2.25 kg bags—and almost always organic. The difference in cost is minimal and the benefits of organic are significant. The skin is thin enough to leave on, especially when eating cooked carrots, and contains a lot of nutritional benefits; buying organic ensures you're not consuming pesticide residue. Also, large bags of organic carrots often have a mix of large and small carrots (conventional carrots tend to be of uniform size). I use the larger carrots for roasting and for cutting into fries, and the smaller ones for snacking.

I avoid pre-shredded carrots or baby carrots, as they're washed in a solution to preserve them. When cutting up raw carrots for snacking, I do peel them. For this, I enlist the help of the kids, giving everyone a bowl and kid-safe peelers and turning on the TV. With everyone working together, we can peel a 5-pound/2.25 kg bag of carrots before a thirty-minute show is over.

GARLIC

Garlic is an essential and inexpensive ingredient. I use it in the majority of my cooking. I prefer fresh heads of garlic over prepeeled garlic. If you find chopping garlic tedious, I suggest doing it all in one go—peel and chop a whole head, then store it in a couple of tablespoons of vegetable oil in an airtight container in your refrigerator for up to 3 days. However, I don't recommend buying brined prechopped garlic, which can have an acrid flavor that will do more harm than good to your cooking.

GINGER

A small amount of ginger goes a very long way. Some people like to scrape off the peel of any extra ginger and freeze it for later use, but I prefer it fresh. There is a certain structural change that comes from the freezing and thawing process that deadens the flavor, so buy only what you need. For a similar reason, I almost never use ground ginger in cooking. I'm passionate about this zesty little rhizome and encourage you to experiment with it, either in place of garlic or alongside it.

GREEN ONIONS

Also known as scallions, green onions work across many different types of cuisines. I use the whole vegetable except the root. The green part is mellower and herbier, like a cross between an onion and parsley. The white part has a stronger flavor, closer to a white onion. The white part works well as a garnish, and the greens, while also great as a garnish, are delicious thrown into stocks and baked dishes.

JALAPEÑOS

I love jalapeños! They're easy to find, easy to use, and incredibly inexpensive; I recently paid a mere $0.02 for a jalapeño on sale.

If you want to preserve the heat of the chile, leave the seeds and white membranes intact; if you want a milder flavor, remove them. Cooking jalapeños also reduces their spiciness. If you want a smoky flavor, you can char them over a gas burner, in a grill pan, or on a grill. For double smokiness, I roast them in bacon fat. This brings out a delicious smoky flavor that is reminiscent of chipotle peppers, which are, in fact, smoked jalapeños.

LEMONS

Lemons show up in so many of the things I make. I use the juice in sauces and the zest as a finisher or as an element of breading. If you don't have lemons on hand, a lime can provide brightness and acidity, even though their flavors are different.

I like to juice lemons and freeze the juice in ice cube trays. The grated zest can be dried and stored in an airtight container, but nothing will ever taste as good as fresh.

When cooking with lemons, just remember one important rule: Don't use the white part of the lemon (called the pith), because it is incredibly bitter. When zesting, take care to avoid the pith; the multipurpose Microplane (which I also use for chocolate, ginger, garlic, other citrus, and onions) is great for this. It's much better and easier than using a box grater.

If you're a next-level lemon fan, you can even cook with lemon segments. They will add a lot of texture and flavor to your recipes, but be sure to remove the membrane covering the segments and any seeds.

MUSHROOMS

Mushrooms are a useful ingredient in vegetarian dishes, especially when you're looking for a "meaty" texture. But I love adding them anywhere and everywhere because they remind me of all things Stroganoff and of Philly cheesesteak. I usually buy brown button or cremini mushrooms, because I think they have more flavor. Whether you buy presliced mushrooms, which are a huge time-saver, or whole, use mushrooms within a week, or they'll become slimy.

When cooking mushrooms, take care to not crowd them in your pan, and give them 3 to 4 minutes of undisturbed cooking before stirring or flipping. That way you'll get a nice sear and a delicious roasted flavor, rather than steamed, limp mushrooms.

When using mushrooms in braised dishes, I add them to the pot during the last 30 to 45 minutes of cooking. They break down considerably during cooking and adding them earlier will cause them to fall apart.

ONIONS

Yellow onions caramelize beautifully, making them a great base for stews and braises. Red onions are amazing roasted and will add a delicate sweetness to a dish. As they brown in the oven, they take on an almost jam-like consistency.

SWEET POTATOES

I keep sweet potatoes in the pantry all year round. They're super-healthy, cook up nicely in stews and soups, and make delicious fries. They're also great roasted alongside other root vegetables, like parsnips and turnips.

Whether or not to keep the skin on can be a point of contention, but stay with me. If I'm making a hash where the sweet potatoes are cut into a small (½-inch/13 mm) dice, I leave the skin on to preserve those nutrients and give the dish a little more texture. I make sure to scrub the potatoes first. When they'll be served in wedges or larger chunks, I will peel them, since a large piece of skin can be tough.

Sweet potatoes vary dramatically in shape and size. I prefer tube-shaped sweet potatoes over rounder ones. They tend to be more evenly shaped and are easier to cut through.

POTATOES

When I need potatoes for a recipe, I almost always reach for Yukon Gold. They're thin-skinned, which means I don't need to peel them, saving time and allowing me to keep those extra nutrients. The texture of Yukon Gold is creamy, buttery, and rich. They are slightly sweeter than russet potatoes and the flesh is moister, which means you'll need less heavy cream or butter when making mashed potatoes. Yukons are also great for roasting; the outside will crisp up and the middle will stay fluffy. These are all wins! The only down side? The extra moisture means that they don't get as crispy as I like for homemade French fries, so I stick to russets for those.

Baking

PIE DOUGH

I know making pie dough causes anxiety in many; it can seem tempermental and hard to handle, but I have a few tricks to make the process nearly fail-safe. I use a food processor to do the hard work for me, and I use butter that I've frozen and diced so I don't run the risk of warming up the butter too much while processing the dough. Then I chill the dough thoroughly before rolling it out. You can, of course, use a prepared piecrust (it's easy to find high-quality ones these days; I like Immaculate Baking or Pillsbury), but for super-flaky homemade dough, use this recipe.

Makes enough for 2 (10-inch/25 cm) pies or 1 (10-inch/25 cm) double-crust pie

2½ cups/320 g all-purpose flour

1 teaspoon sugar

1 teaspoon salt

16 Tablespoons (2 sticks)/225 g unsalted butter, frozen and diced

½ cup/120 ml cold water

1 In a food processor, pulse the flour, sugar, and salt together for a couple of seconds. Add the butter cubes, then slowly add the water through the feed tube, pulsing until the mixture forms pea-sized pieces.

2 Take the dough out of the processor and knead it together just a couple of times to form a rough ball.

3 Cut the dough into 2 pieces and shape each one into a disc. Wrap tightly with

plastic wrap. Refrigerate for at least an hour and up to a day before using.

PUFF PASTRY

While puff pastry is marginally more expensive than store-bought piecrust, it's more versatile, because it can be used for savory foods as well as desserts. It is easier to work with than pie dough, and you can even use it to make the perfect one-ingredient snack: puff pastry cut into slices, baked, and eaten warm. Brushed with an egg wash and sprinkled with coarse sanding sugar, you can make *palmiers*. Or, baked with the addition of jam, Nutella, lemon curd, fruit, or cream cheese, it can be used in any number of quick desserts.

SHELF-STABLE PANTRY STAPLES

After many years of overbuying, I've honed my list of essential pantry items to these. Sure, there are other things I'll pick up on a whim or to try out a new recipe, but these are the basic items I turn to most often.

Dry Goods

ALL-PURPOSE FLOUR

The flour used for all the recipes in this book is standard all-purpose. I always transfer the flour from the bag to an airtight container to keep it fresh and bug-free. I also keep the container out of direct sunlight, because light and heat can contribute to spoilage.

When measuring flour for baking, use a clean spoon to scoop the flour into a measuring cup, then level it off. Simply dipping your measuring cup into the flour container can give an inaccurate measurement and also result in cross-contamination.

BAKING POWDER

Baking powder is a leavening agent. Unlike baking soda (see below), baking powder also contains an acid, so it only requires the addition of a liquid to activate it. Baking powder should be replaced every 12 months. Test whether it is still active by adding some water to it and stirring. If it does not bubble up immediately, it should to be replaced.

BAKING SODA

Baking soda is another leavening agent that is used to help baked goods rise. It requires an acid and a liquid to activate it. Once the container has been opened, be sure to replace it every 12 months. To test whether it is still active, put a spoonful of baking soda into a bowl and add vinegar. If the baking soda fizzes, it is still good.

While baking soda is a good refrigerator deodorizer, it's never a good idea to use

Bulk Bins

Buying from bulk bins (not to be confused with buying in bulk!) is one of the best tricks to keeping a right-sized pantry. Spices, nuts, and flours are all ingredients that typically come in packages too large to go through quickly enough before they lose their potency. Bulk food sections are a great way to both save a little money and avoid large containers that can overwhelm your pantry. With bulk bins, you can often buy spices in quantities as small as a tablespoon, meaning that experimenting with new flavors doesn't have to incur the expense of a whole jar that will inevitably go stale. Same with nuts, so if a recipe calls for ¼ cup/40 g of peanuts, you can buy just that amount.

In my town, Sprouts and Winco are the best places to find well-priced bulk spices and dry goods, with enough turnover to know that I'm getting the freshest ingredients. I've invested in small jars for spices, medium ones for nuts, and large canisters for pasta, flours, and sugar. I transfer my bulk-bin items to these when I get home from the store.

the opened box in your fridge in recipes, because it will have absorbed odors.

CORNSTARCH

Cornstarch is a naturally gluten-free thickening agent. In addition to soups, sauces, and pie fillings it can be used to create a crispy coating when frying.

To thicken sauces, soups, or pie fillings, mix the cornstarch with cold or room-temperature water (hot will cause it to clump) to create a slurry.

SALT

I use two kinds of salt in my cooking: kosher salt for savory cooking and iodized table salt for baking.

I switched to kosher salt for cooking after taking a class on salt in culinary school. We taste-tested twelve different salts for both cooking and finishing a dish. While kosher salt has larger crystals, table salt is actually saltier. The reason: The pressurization that is required to create the smaller crystals in table salt makes it significantly more sodium packed by volume. Kosher salt gives me the ability to add salt throughout the cooking process without running the risk of oversalting my food. If you are not using kosher salt, I recommend using half to two-thirds the amount of salt called for in my recipes.

I use table salt for baking because its smaller crystals allow it to be incorporated more evenly into a mixture, and it also dissolves more quickly.

PANKO

I used to think of panko as just the breading you'd find on tempura, but I now use it in place of bread crumbs to make a light and crispy coating for all kinds of foods. The signature difference between panko and bread crumbs is its aerated texture and prominent crunch.

Panko can also be toasted with butter and cheese and used as a crispy topping for mac and cheese or seared fish.

TOMATOES

Canned tomatoes are the easiest, most inexpensive way to ensure that you have tomatoes to use year-round. There are good uses for diced and crushed tomatoes: Here is my guide for deciding on what is best used and when. Regardless of which type I'm using, I always buy the organic version because they're not much more expensive, and it ensures there weren't chemicals used in growing the tomatoes, or in peeling them—which is a concern when you buy low priced, non-organic canned tomato products.

Crushed tomatoes are a great alternative to tomato sauce because they have more body and texture. They work well in chilis, marinara sauces, braised meats, and pizza sauces.

Diced tomatoes are a great way to add thickness and flavor to soups and roasts. The tomato liquid takes the place of water in a recipe. I'll opt for seasoned diced tomatoes to add a little more flavor instead of fresh herbs when I'm short on time or ingredients.

Like Better Than Bouillon (see page 35), *tomato paste* offers a boost of flavor without adding extra liquid. It can be stirred into creamy sauces for another layer of flavor, or even to commercial spaghetti sauces to make them taste a little more homemade. Tomato paste adds an umami quality to dishes without adding any fat. You can deepen the flavor of tomato paste by lightly cooking it with onions in olive oil before turning that into a sauce base.

Tomato paste is available in cans or tubes. The tubes are convenient because they can be resealed and stored in the fridge. However, they're also significantly more expensive per ounce. I often buy a six-ounce/170 g can and spread the contents out evenly in a large freezer bag. Once frozen, you can simply break off as much tomato paste as you need and add it your heated pan.

Sauces and Condiments

GREEN CURRY PASTE

Thai green curry paste, sold in small cans or jars, is a mixture of garlic, ginger, chilies, makrut lime, lemongrass, and sweeteners. It's a quick and flavorful base for stir-fries, soups, or braised dishes. I add it by the spoonful to give a boost of flavor to a dish. With a can of coconut milk, a protein, and some veggies, it makes an easy curry.

HOISIN SAUCE

Hoisin sauce is a thick, sweet glaze made from fermented soybeans. I use it in stir-fries, braises, or as a glaze for grilled meats and veggies. I keep a jar of it next to our favorite barbecue sauces in the fridge. I like the Lee Kum Kee and Soy Vay brands.

HOT SAUCE

Hot sauce really deserves its own chapter— there are so many varieties that I love.

Tabasco is a potent thin sauce, Tapatío is a bit thicker and milder. When a recipe in this book calls for hot sauce, Tapatío is a good choice, but feel free to experiment to find one with the flavor and level of heat that best suits you (see Sriracha, page 30).

MARINARA SAUCE

Once you find a brand of marinara sauce you like, keep your eyes open for when it goes on sale and then buy a few jars. I like Muir Glen and Newman's Own because they're high-quality and also well priced. I steer clear of ones with chunks of vegetables, because I prefer to add cut-up fresh vegetables, but the sauces flavored with roasted garlic or herbs are sure bets.

MUSTARD

Dijon mustard adds a lot of flavor without a lot of calories. It also acts as an emulsifier if you're making a vinaigrette or a marinade. It's slightly bolder and less tangy than yellow mustard. It keeps indefinitely in the fridge once opened.

I often mix classic **yellow mustard** into sauces for sloppy joes or toppings for meatloaf. And, of course, it's a natural for burgers and fries.

PLUM SAUCE

Plum sauce is a canned or jarred sweet-and-sour sauce, often served as a dipping sauce for egg rolls, pot stickers, or other dim sum. When it is exposed to heat in a skillet or as a glaze roasted in an oven, the sugars caramelize, giving an even deeper flavor to the sauce.

SOY SAUCE

I use soy sauce a lot for sauces and marinades. And while I normally love full-flavored ingredients, I always opt for low-sodium soy sauce. Since soy sauce is typically one of several ingredients in a sauce or marinade, the low-sodium variety allows me to better control the overall saltiness of the dish. If you use regular soy sauce in place of low-sodium in any of the recipes in this book, you may need to cut down on the salt elsewhere.

SRIRACHA

Sriracha is a smooth garlic-based hot pepper sauce. It is potent and quite spicy, so be careful with the amount you add. In fact, when you first start using it, I'd recommend using half the amount called for in the recipe, tasting, and then adjusting the amount as desired.

Herbs and Spices

BAY LEAVES

Bay leaves are essential for building flavor in recipes. Do not omit them! These dried leaves (which you should always remove before serving) add an underlying savory element as well as depth of flavor. Always buy dried bay leaves, never fresh, which lack the depth of flavor. I generally pick up a small handful from a bulk bin, which are significantly less expensive than the jars or tins of leaves.

BLACK PEPPER

Black pepper can have different potencies depending on the coarseness of the grind. I find that a coarser grind distributes the flavor more evenly in a dish. There are many fancy pepper grinders on the market, but

Spices

Spices are some of the most delicate items in the pantry. For optimal flavor, I recommend replacing them every six months. This can get expensive if you're buying full jars of spices, but there is a more economical way. Many grocery stores sell spices in the bulk food section, so you can purchase smaller quantities, then transfer them to small glass jars when you get home. Buying them this way also means you'll have brighter, more full-flavored food because you're not using old spices.

I swear by my $2 Trader Joe's black pepper with its own built-in grinder.

CAYENNE PEPPER

Cayenne comes in different levels of spiciness. Some brands are bright red in color with a high level of spice. Others are a more muted brown-orange in color with a lower level of heat. Look for one that is bright red and boldly spiced. Although you can always use less, it's best to start with one that is more potent.

DRIED OREGANO

Dried oregano is such a useful herb that I typically buy it by the bag. This makes it much more cost effective than buying those small jars, and then I don't run out as quickly. Look for bags of dried oregano in the Mexican food aisle of your grocery store or specialty market.

GROUND CORIANDER

Coriander, like cumin (the two work very nicely together), is highly versatile, used in everything from traditional grilling rubs to Mexican dishes to Middle Eastern and Asian food. This is a spice that deserves space in your pantry.

GROUND CUMIN

Cumin can be used in recipes from cuisines all around the world, from Mexican to Mediterranean. It has a warm flavor, not at all spicy, and I've found that when it is used with other flavors to balance it, it is actually quite kid-friendly.

GROUND GINGER

Ground ginger is boldly flavored and benefits from a light touch. A small amount goes a long way, so most recipes call for less than a teaspoon. While it can be used in both savory and sweet recipes, I prefer it for baking and stick to fresh ginger for cooking. If you are substituting ground ginger for fresh, a good rule of thumb is ¼ teaspoon ground for 1 tablespoon minced fresh ginger.

PAPRIKA

I use classic paprika, not smoked, hot, or spicy. It adds a sweetness and bright red color to many dishes. A pinch of paprika is not going to change the overall flavor of your dish like a pinch of cayenne would, but it adds a nice dimension.

SPICE MIXES
(Jerk, Old Bay, Taco, and Cajun Seasoning)

Spice mixes are some of my favorite cooking cheats. You can, of course, make your own (and I have recipes for all of these on my website), but premixed jars save a lot of time.

I use these mixes most frequently for roasted vegetables or grilled meats. Adding a dash of Cajun seasoning to roasted potatoes, peppers, and onions will give them a whole new life and help prevent "side dish fatigue."

THYME (fresh and dried)

Thyme is an essential component of any roast meat I make. Since I use both fresh and dried thyme, I usually buy it fresh and then dry whatever is left over; see the Tip below.

TIP: *To dry thyme, you can tie the sprigs together and hang them upside down in a cool place until dried. Or place the sprigs in the microwave between layers of paper towels and microwave in 15-second increments until they're completely dried.*

Chocolate and Cocoa Powder

CHOCOLATE

Chocolate chips, discs, and bars are all important ingredients in my baking.

Chocolate chips are great for cookies (of course), brownies, and other desserts where you want the chocolate bits to hold their shape rather than melt; they often don't melt at high temperatures. Look for high-quality chocolate chips on sale and stock up then. To keep their shape, they also contain less cocoa butter than other types of chocolate, which makes tempering chocolate chips almost impossible without adding additional fat, and if you try to make a sauce with chocolate chips you'll end up with a streaky (and usually bloomed) finish.

For melting chocolate, I use *chocolate discs* or *baking bars*. I usually seek out Guittard because it melts well and is inexpensive relative to its high quality. You can buy chocolate discs in the bulk-bin section or by the box. If you're using baking bars, carefully cut them into small shards with

a chef's knife before melting the chocolate. For discs, or the cut shards of baking bars, you can simply warm them gently in your microwave in 30-second increments until melted, then gently stir.

Unsweetened Cocoa Powder: Cocoa powder makes for delicious brownies and cakes. I usually buy Ghirardelli, which is flavorful and easy to find. When I want a richer, bolder flavor, I'll use Hershey's Special Dark cocoa powder.

Pasta and Grains

PASTA

Traditionally, in Italian cooking, specific pasta shapes are matched with specific types of sauces. But I don't have any hard-and-fast rules when it comes to choosing pasta shapes; ultimately it's a matter of personal preference. My only recommendation is to always cook your pasta one minute shy of the directions on the box. There will be carryover cooking after you drain it, and if you cook it as long as directed on the package, the pasta will be overcooked.

NOTE: *I call for heavily salting pasta cooking water—1 tablespoon per each quart of water. Well-salted water helps flavor the pasta evenly. I don't recommend rinsing pasta with water after cooking, since that would remove some of the starch that will help thicken any sauce you top it with. If you find your pasta is sticking together, you can toss the pasta with just a bit of oil, which will also prevent it from absorbing too much sauce and getting mushy.*

RICE

For most recipes, I use long-grain rice, the standard variety you'll find in your local grocery store. However, a few years ago (when I became a mom) I started pushing for more whole grains in our household. Now I cook with more brown rice and find that making brown rice with stock in place of water is my go-to.

Before cooking white or brown rice, I rinse the rice in a sieve under cold water until the water runs clear to remove excess starch. If I want the rice to have a less sticky texture, I will sometimes sauté the grains in just a tablespoon of oil, until the rice turns white, and then boil it. My favorite trick with rice though, is to bake it. Over the years I've had my fair share of unevenly cooked rice, and since moving to baked rice I've found it's not only more delicious but just about failproof.

Nuts and Legumes

PEANUTS

Buying unsalted roasted peanuts allows me to use the nuts in both sweet and savory recipes. If I want to salt the peanuts for a recipe, I simply add some kosher or iodized salt to a small food processor and pulse it fifteen to twenty times until the salt is finer, almost the texture of powdered sugar, then toss the nuts with as much of the salt as needed.

OTHER NUTS

Nuts should be kept in airtight containers and either used within 3 months or stored in the freezer. Otherwise, the natural oils in the nuts will cause them to go rancid.

PEANUT BUTTER

I have two modes when it comes to peanut butter. For our day-to-day peanut butter and jelly sandwich-making needs, it's all natural all the way. But for cooking or baking, conventional no-stir, creamy peanut butter is far superior. The latter stays emulsified, whereas natural peanut butter will *naturally* separate, making for a lumpy sauce or a heavy, dense batter.

TIP: *Using chunky rather than smooth peanut butter when making a sauce gives you the texture of chopped peanuts in your sauce without adding another ingredient.*

Sweeteners

SUGAR

I use light brown sugar. Dark brown sugar has more molasses, so if you substitute that, the flavor will be a bit deeper and bolder. In some recipes that can be delicious, but in recipes for vegetables or meat, the flavor can be overwhelming. Pack brown sugar into the measuring cup to measure it.

Store brown sugar in an airtight container to prevent it from hardening. You can add a slice of bread or a terra cotta stone to absorb moisture from the air and keep your brown sugar moist.

White sugar will sweeten your recipes without the additional flavor of brown sugar. When measuring white sugar, level off the measuring cup or spoon with a knife.

HONEY

Honey is a very flavorful sweetener and you only need a small amount to make a big impact on your cooking. There are many types of honey—so find the one you like. Just be sure it's authentic honey and not sweetened syrup.

Oils and Fats

BAKING SPRAY

In addition to using a vegetable oil spray, I sometimes use baking spray for dessert recipes. Baking spray is a mixture of butter or oil and flour that comes in an aerosol can. It can take the place of greasing and flouring a baking pan.

EXTRA-VIRGIN OLIVE OIL

Extra-virgin olive oil is great for both cooking and for finishing a dish. Buy it from a store you trust and avoid "blended" olive oils, which can contain any number of other oils in any ratio. Costco and Whole Foods are both great sources for fairly priced high-quality olive oil.

SESAME OIL

Sesame oil is an intensely flavored oil that is best used in small quantities, usually no more than a tablespoon per recipe. I add it to stir-fries, sauces, dressings, and marinades.

Look for pure sesame oil, not a blend. Toasted and untoasted sesame oil can be used interchangeably in the recipes in this book.

VEGETABLE OIL

This is my go-to neutral oil for cooking when I don't want to add another flavor. Vegetable oil is a processed blend of a number of different oils. It doesn't have the nutrients and health benefits of olive oil. However, it does have a high smoke point (400°F/205°C).

It is inexpensive (both the organic and conventional versions), and it is a workhorse in my pantry.

Additional Condiments

BALSAMIC VINEGAR

As with honey and olive oil, shopping for balsamic vinegar requires a discerning eye. The best balsamic vinegar is made from grape pressings that are boiled down into a syrup and aged for at least twelve years in wood barrels. The production is tightly monitored, and because it's a time-consuming process, the price reflects that. You don't typically use much at any one time, so it pays to get a high-quality bottle; be sure that it is authentic balsamic and hasn't been mixed with other vinegars. I like the Trader Joe's brand because it's inexpensive and has just enough sweetness to counteract the natural acidity of vinegar. Balsamic vinegar can be used in both cooked and uncooked dishes.

BETTER THAN BOUILLON

Better Than Bouillon is a concentrated flavor base, like bouillon cubes, but it comes in a jar, so it's easy to scoop out just as much as you'd like. I use Better Than Bouillon in place of broth and stock in my kitchen, and it's a quick way to add a punch of flavor to a dish, as you might use a bouillon cube. I use 1 heaping teaspoon per cup/235 ml of liquid (more than the directions call for) of Roasted Chicken Better Than Bouillon (which is organic) for a flavorful broth replacement.

When I want to add chicken flavor to a recipe, I use it straight from the jar. Stirring 1 teaspoon into a skillet sauce or 1 tablespoon to a pot of braising liquid adds a great base of flavor (as well as sodium, so don't salt the dish until after you add the BTB).

Since I cook every day, oftentimes for large crowds, and am often experimenting with new recipes, I also keep BTB Roasted Beef, Mushroom, Vegetable, Lobster, and Fish flavors on hand. I keep my BTB in the fridge after opening.

COCONUT MILK

With a deep flavor and creamy consistency, coconut milk is a delicious addition to sauces. It can also be used as a shelf-stable substitute for heavy cream. I avoid light coconut milk, because it lacks the texture and thickness of the full-fat version. If you're cutting back on fat for dietary reasons and opt for light coconut milk, you may need to use an additional thickener, like cornstarch or tapioca starch, to your dish.

TIP: *Try whipping coconut milk into soft peaks to use as a garnish with fruity desserts like Key lime pie. Just refrigerate the coconut milk until very cold, then whip the solidified cream, adding just a tablespoon or two of powdered sugar and a teaspoon of vanilla extract.*

Part 2

RECIPES

3 *Ingredient* DINNERS

SAUSAGE AND FENNEL PASTA

Sausage and fennel pasta is dear to my heart: It was one of the first meals I made for my husband when we started dating. He loved it so much that it's still in steady rotation in our house all these years later. The Italian sausage does a lot of the heavy lifting in this recipe, because it has so much built-in seasoning, which means you can achieve a very flavorful dish with fewer ingredients. This is flavor-packed as it is, but if you'd like to serve it with some grated Parmesan cheese on top, that would be delicious. *Serves 6*

Kosher salt

1 pound/455 g orecchiette

1 tablespoon vegetable oil, plus more for the pasta

1 pound/455 g Italian sausage, sweet or spicy

1 bulb fennel, trimmed and thinly sliced, reserving fennel fronds for garnish if desired

¼ teaspoon coarsely ground black pepper

NOTE: *If you don't feel like cooking this in a skillet, you can toss the sausage and sliced fennel on a sheet pan and roast them at 375°F/190°C for 18 to 20 minutes.*

1 Bring a large pot of heavily salted water to a boil. Add the pasta and cook for 1 minute shy of the package directions. Drain, transfer to a bowl, and toss with oil to keep the pasta from sticking; set aside.

2 Slice open the casings of the sausage and remove the ground pork.

3 Heat the oil in a large skillet over medium-high heat. Once it's hot, add the sausage and cook, stirring occasionally, for 4 to 5 minutes, until well browned.

4 Remove the sausage from the pan with a slotted spoon and set aside. Add the sliced fennel to the pan, along with the pepper and salt to taste and cook for 3 to 4 minutes, until the fennel is softened.

5 Add the pasta and sausage to the pan and toss to heat through. Serve.

SUBSTITUTIONS

Orecchiete	1 pound/455 g ziti	4 cups/852 g mashed potatoes
Italian Sausage	4 boneless, skinless chicken thighs, cut into chunks	1 pound/455 g andouille sausage
Fresh Fennel	1 teaspoon fennel seeds	2 red or green bell peppers, cored, seeded, and sliced

Letting Your Oil Properly Heat

Hot oil provides a protective barrier so foods don't stick to the pan. Adding ingredients like meat or fish before the oil has properly heated will cause them to stick and burn rather than getting a nice sear. For vegetables, adding them before the oil is hot will cause them to absorb more of the oil, making them greasy and soggy. To test if the oil is hot, drop a tiny bit of whatever you're cooking into the pan and make sure it sizzles.

SPICY SAUSAGE HASH

This is one of those unicorn recipes that is good for any meal of the day, can be made in a snap and eaten right away, but can also be made ahead and frozen for later. My family devours this dish, so we rarely have leftovers, but when we do, I use them with scrambled eggs and cheese to make the best-ever breakfast burritos. *Serves 4*

1 pound/455 g
Yukon Gold potatoes,
scrubbed and diced

1 pound/455 g spicy
Italian sausage, sliced

1 red bell pepper,
cored, seeded, and
diced

1 tablespoon unsalted
butter (optional)

1 teaspoon kosher salt

¼ teaspoon coarsely
ground black pepper

1 Bring a large pot of water to a boil. Add the potatoes and parboil for 8 to 10 minutes. Drain, pat dry, and set aside.

2 Add the sausage to a medium skillet and cook over medium heat to render the fat. (Be sure to keep the heat at medium so the sausage cooks slowly and doesn't burn.)

3 Remove the sausage from the pan with a slotted spoon and set aside. Add the bell pepper and potatoes. If you'd prefer a bit more fat, add the butter. Season with the salt and pepper.

4 Turn up the heat to medium-high and cook for 5 to 6 minutes, until the potatoes and peppers are crispy.

5 Return the sausage to the pan and stir to combine.

SUBSTITUTIONS

Yukon Gold Potatoes	1 pound/455 g red potatoes
Spicy Italian Sausages	4 bone-in, skin-on chicken thighs, seasoned with ½ teaspoon Italian seasoning and crushed red pepper, cut into cubes after cooking
Bell Pepper	2 cloves garlic, minced

BROWN SUGAR PORK CHOPS

This brown sugar marinade was a revelation for me! It can be used for chops (as I've done here) or for stir-fries with your favorite vegetables. The soy sauce and brown sugar just need a few minutes to work their magic and flavor the pork, so there's no need for advance planning. Just be sure to wipe off as much of the marinade as possible before cooking to allow the pork to sear and prevent burning. This marinade has replaced all the bottled marinades I used to keep in my fridge, because it is so easy and quick. *Serves 4*

¼ teaspoon kosher salt

¼ teaspoon coarsely ground black pepper

3 tablespoons low-sodium soy sauce

½ cup/110 g packed light brown sugar

4 (1-inch/2.5 cm thick) pork loin chops (1¾ to 2 pounds/ 795 to 910 g total)

4 tablespoons vegetable oil

1 In a large bowl, combine the salt, pepper, soy sauce, and brown sugar and whisk into a slurry. Add the pork chops and turn to coat well. Cover with plastic wrap and let sit for 20 minutes.

2 Heat a large heavy skillet over medium-high heat, then add 2 tablespoons of the vegetable oil. Once the oil is hot, dab off any excess marinade from the pork with paper towels and add the pork chops to the pan. Cook the pork until nicely browned on the first side, 4 to 5 minutes. Add the remaining 2 tablespoons oil and give it a few seconds to heat, then flip the pork chops and brown on the other side, another 4 to 5 minutes. Transfer the pork chops to a plate.

3 Add the remaining marinade from the bowl to the skillet and allow it to thicken for several minutes. Serve the chops with the sauce drizzled over the top.

SUBSTITUTIONS

Pork Chops	4 bone-in, skin-on chicken thighs

GARLIC-HONEY CHICKEN

Quick stir-fries are a weeknight lifesaver. My kids love this dish, and I make it a few times a month—at least! The garlic and honey are strong enough on their own, but you can also treat this as a base to build on; sometimes I give it an Asian flair with just a spoonful of soy sauce, other times I squeeze over some lemon and add olives for a Mediterranean flavor. *Serves 4*

3 boneless, skinless chicken breasts

½ teaspoon kosher salt

¼ teaspoon coarsely ground black pepper

3 tablespoons vegetable oil

4 cloves garlic, minced

¼ cup/60 ml honey

1 Slice the chicken into strips roughly 1 inch/2.5 cm wide. Season with the salt and pepper.

2 Heat half the oil in a large skillet over medium-high heat. Once the oil is hot, add half of the chicken and let it sear for 2 minutes, without stirring, then flip the chicken over and cook for another 2 minutes. Remove the chicken and set aside.

3 Add the remaining oil to the skillet and repeat the process with the second half of the chicken.

4 Once the second batch is cooked through, keep it in the pan, and add the garlic. Cook for 30 seconds, until the garlic becomes fragrant.

5 Return the first batch of cooked chicken to the pan, add 1 tablespoon water and the honey, and stir for about 30 seconds to coat the chicken.

SUBSTITUTIONS

Chicken Breasts	4 (6-ounce/170 g) salmon fillets	2 pounds/910 g (13–15 count) shrimp, peeled and deveined
Garlic	4 slices bacon, chopped	2 teaspoons minced fresh ginger
Honey	¼ cup/55 g packed light brown sugar	¼ cup/60 ml maple syrup

CITRUS SALMON

This recipe couldn't be easier to pull together. Any other citrus you happen to have on hand can be substituted for the lemon, and the result will be just as delicious and bright. I think this dish is perfect as is, but if you want some sweetness, a drizzle of honey at the end is a wonderful addition. *Serves 4*

2 tablespoons olive oil

4 (6-ounce/170 g) salmon fillets, skin on

½ teaspoon kosher salt

¼ teaspoon coarsely ground black pepper

3 cloves garlic, minced

Grated zest and juice of 1 lemon (about 3 tablespoons juice)

1 Add the olive oil to a medium skillet set over medium heat.

2 Season the salmon with the salt and pepper. Once the oil is hot, add the salmon skin side down and cook for 4 to 5 minutes. Flip the salmon and cook for another 3 to 4 minutes.

3 Add the garlic to the skillet and cook for 10 seconds. Add the lemon zest and juice and remove from the heat.

4 Serve the salmon with the lemon sauce drizzled over each fillet.

SUBSTITUTIONS

Salmon	2 pounds/910 g (13–15 count) shrimp, peeled and deveined	4 boneless, skinless chicken breasts
Garlic	2 teaspoons minced fresh ginger	2 tablespoons sweet chili sauce
Lemon (zest and juice)	Grated zest and juice of 1 lime	Grated zest and juice of ½ orange

BROWN-BUTTER COD

I love this recipe because the result looks and tastes like a fancy restaurant dish, but it uses one of the most economical varieties of fish. The secret: brown butter. Simply cooking butter until it browns transforms it into a very nuanced and nutty base for the mild-flavored fish. Brown butter lends such a lovely warm flavor that can be used in many recipes. Simply tossing noodles in it makes for a simple vegetarian (and kid-friendly) meal. *Serves 4*

4 (6-ounce/170 g) cod fillets, skin on

¼ teaspoon kosher salt

¼ teaspoon coarsely ground black pepper

8 tablespoons (1 stick)/113 g unsalted butter

Juice of 1 lemon (about 3 tablespoons)

2 tablespoons capers, drained

1 Season the cod fillets with the salt and pepper.

2 Place the butter in a large pan set over medium heat. (Using a stainless steel or enamel-coated frying pan rather than a dark pan will allow you to see when the butter browns.)

3 When the butter has melted, add the cod skin side down and cook for 4 to 5 minutes, then flip. Cook for another 3 minutes, then remove the fish and set aside.

4 Raise the heat to medium-high. When the butter begins to brown and you can see the butter solids separating from the clear liquid in the pan, add the lemon juice and capers and turn off the heat.

5 Whisk the sauce well and drizzle over the fish.

SUBSTITUTIONS

Cod	4 (6-ounce/170 g) tilapia fillets
Lemon Juice	¼ cup/60 ml white wine
Capers	¼ cup/13 g chopped fresh tarragon

Classic Recipe
EASY-BREEZY POT ROAST

Ina Garten's Company Pot Roast is one of my all-time favorite recipes. It's really the perfect dish. For years it was on heavy rotation when I cooked for families as a private chef. I love it so much that I wanted to find a way to re-create that same tender, succulent roast for my own family without the long list of ingredients to prep. After some trial and error, I settled on using a jarred marinara sauce. This shortcut works because the marinara sauce has all of the cooked aromatics built in. The red wine elevates the flavors and adds a beautiful sophistication to the roast.

With so few ingredients, make sure they are good ones. I like Newman's Own and Rao's marinara sauces. A full-bodied red like a Cabernet works best here; choose one that you enjoy drinking. Serve over mashed potatoes or polenta; it also pairs well with mac and cheese. (See photo of finished dish on cover and page 29.) *Serves 8*

1 (5-pound/2.3 kg) chuck roast

2 teaspoons kosher salt

½ teaspoon coarsely ground black pepper

2 tablespoons vegetable oil

1 (24-ounce/680 g) jar marinara sauce

2 cups/475 ml red wine

TIP: *If you'd prefer to cook this in the slow cooker, omit the water and cook on low for 8 hours.*

1 Preheat the oven to 325°F/165°C (or use a slow cooker; see Tip).

2 Season the chuck roast with the salt and pepper.

3 Heat the oil in a large Dutch oven over medium-high heat. Once the oil is hot, add the chuck roast and sear on all sides until a dark brown crust forms, 6 to 8 minutes per side.

4 Turn the heat down to medium-low, add the marinara sauce, red wine, and 2 cups/475 ml water, and stir well.

5 Cover the Dutch oven, transfer to the oven, and cook for 2½ to 3 hours, until the meat is fork-tender.

SUBSTITUTIONS

Chuck Roast	4 pounds/1.8 kg boneless short ribs	1 (4-pound/1.8 kg) pork loin roast
Marinara Sauce	¼ cup/60 ml tomato paste, 1 (28-ounce/795 g) can diced tomatoes, and 2 cups/475 ml chicken broth	no change to recipe
Red Wine	2 cups/475 ml grape juice	no change to recipe

BRAISED CHICKEN WITH BACON AND BEER

This is a hearty meal, perfect for a cozy night in. The beer gives it a flavor reminiscent of your favorite pub dish and helps break down any tough parts of the chicken, making it extremely tender. For the best flavor, I cook the bacon first and use the rendered fat to give the chicken an initial sear.

I serve this over cheesy mashed potatoes, but any creamy starch will do. If you're looking for game-day meal ideas, you can turn it into a sub by shredding the cooked chicken, melting provolone over it, and serving that in a roll. *Serves 4*

4 bone-in, skin-on chicken thighs

1 teaspoon kosher salt

¼ teaspoon coarsely ground black pepper

8 slices bacon

1 (12-ounce/355 ml) bottle dark lager

1 Preheat the oven to 350°F/175°C.

2 Pat the chicken thighs dry with a paper towel and season with the salt and pepper.

3 Coarsely chop the bacon. Transfer to a large ovenproof skillet set over medium heat and cook until the fat has rendered and the bacon has browned slightly but is not crisp.

4 Using a slotted spoon, transfer the bacon to paper towels to drain, leaving the fat in the pan. If you have much more than 2 tablespoons fat, remove the excess and discard or save for another use.

5 Add the chicken skin side down to the skillet, still over medium heat, and cook undisturbed for 4 to 5 minutes, until the skin is golden brown. Flip gently and cook on the second side for another 4 to 5 minutes, until it's also nicely browned. Add the beer and bring to a simmer.

6 Transfer the pan to the oven and cook, uncovered, for 30 minutes. Most of the liquid will have cooked off and the chicken will be tender. Add the bacon back to the pan and stir well.

SUBSTITUTIONS

Chicken Thighs	4 pounds/1.8 kg boneless short ribs
Beer	1 (12-ounce/355 ml) can root beer or 1 (12-ounce/355 ml) bottle apple juice

TOMATO-BALSAMIC PULLED PORK

This is one of my favorite back-pocket recipes; I always have canned tomatoes and balsamic vinegar on hand, and not only are the ingredients seasonless but the resulting dish works for any gathering you can dream up. Use the pulled pork in tacos or in sandwiches, or serve it over noodles tossed with olive oil—or any starch, for that matter—to soak up the delicious sauce. If you'd like to turn the sauce into a gravy, just transfer it to a saucepan and whisk in a tablespoon each of butter and flour until smooth and well combined.

Balsamic vinegar can vary widely in quality. I've found one that I like at Trader Joe's; it's real balsamic from Italy and is under $10. If your balsamic is on the bitter side, add a teaspoon of sugar to the dish. Otherwise, the acidity of the tomatoes will intensify the bitterness, resulting in a less succulent dish. Any fatty cut of meat will work here, just be sure to brown it first. And, of course, if you want to play around with the flavor, you can always add extras like garlic, caramelized red onion, fennel, or rosemary. *Serves 10*

1 (6-pound/2.7 kg) boneless pork shoulder roast (bone-in would work as well)

2 teaspoons kosher salt

½ teaspoon coarsely ground black pepper

2 tablespoons vegetable oil

¼ cup/60 ml balsamic vinegar

1 (28-ounce/795 g) can diced tomatoes

1 Season the pork with the salt and pepper.

2 Heat the oil in a large Dutch oven or heavy-bottomed pot over medium-high heat. Once the oil is hot, add the pork and brown it well on all sides.

3 Transfer the browned pork to a slow cooker. Mix the vinegar and tomatoes in a medium bowl and pour this over the pork.

4 Cover and cook on low for 8 hours, or until the meat offers no resistance when pricked with a fork.

SUBSTITUTIONS

Pork Shoulder	1 (4-pound/1.8 kg) chuck roast	10 bone-in, skin-on chicken thighs
Balsamic Vinegar	1 cup/235 ml red wine	¼ cup/60 ml bottled balsamic vinaigrette (not creamy)
Diced Tomatoes	1 (28-ounce/795 g) can stewed tomatoes	1 pound/455 g Yukon Gold potatoes, scrubbed and quartered

PINEAPPLE TERIYAKI CHICKEN

God, I love this recipe. Canned pineapple does double duty here: The juice mixes with the soy sauce to caramelize the chicken and create an incredible and nuanced sauce, and the chunks of fruit add some needed texture. The long, slow cooking mellows the saltiness of the soy sauce, and the fat from the chicken thighs adds richness, so you don't end up with salty pineapple juice. The sauce is so good, I've even made it on its own in a saucepan without the chicken. I just whisk in 2 teaspoons cornstarch dissolved in water, to thicken it and let it cook slowly and reduce.

The chicken can be shredded and served with flour tortillas or served over rice with steamed vegetables. *Serves 4*

1 (20-ounce/570 g) can pineapple chunks in juice

⅓ cup/80 ml low-sodium soy sauce

4 bone-in, skin-on chicken thighs

½ teaspoon kosher salt

⅛ teaspoon coarsely ground black pepper

2 tablespoons vegetable oil

1 Preheat the oven to 350°F/175°C.

2 In a medium bowl, mix together the pineapple with juice and soy sauce. Set aside.

3 Season the chicken with salt and pepper.

4 Heat the oil in a large Dutch oven over medium heat. Once the oil is hot, add the chicken skin side down and let it cook, undisturbed, for 4 to 5 minutes, until the fat is rendered and the chicken is nicely browned.

5 Turn the chicken skin side up and add the pineapple–soy sauce mixture. Transfer the Dutch oven to the oven and cook, uncovered, for 20 to 25 minutes. The chicken juices should run clear when pricked with a knife and the sauce should have a syrupy consistency.

SUBSTITUTIONS

Pineapple Chunks in Juice	1 (20-ounce/570 g) jar mango slices in juice	1 (20-ounce/570 g) jar pear slices in juice
Soy Sauce	1 cup/235 ml teriyaki sauce	no change to recipe
Chicken Thighs	4 pounds/1.8 kg boneless short ribs (Increase the cooking time to 3 hours; this will feed 4 to 6 people.)	4 pounds/1.8 kg boneless country-style pork ribs (Increase the cooking time to 3 hours; this will feed 4 to 6 people.)

GARLIC AND BROWN SUGAR CHICKEN

Brown sugar is sweet without being cloying, and it has the ability to tame garlic's bite, mellowing it but not subduing it altogether. Here it has the added superpower of giving the chicken a beautiful caramelization. You can serve this super–kid-friendly meal over rice or in sandwiches, or cut up the chicken and use it in fried rice or stir-fries.

This combination of brown sugar and garlic can be used on *any* protein: chicken breasts, thighs, patties, you name it. You want to cook any of these in the oven, not in a skillet over high heat, though, because the brown sugar would burn. Slow and steady is the way to go. *Serves 4*

4 bone-in, skin-on chicken thighs

2 tablespoons vegetable oil

½ teaspoon kosher salt

⅛ teaspoon coarsely ground black pepper

½ cup/110 g packed light brown sugar

6 cloves garlic, minced

1 Preheat the oven to 375°F/190°C. Line a sheet pan with parchment paper or aluminum foil.

2 Pat the chicken thighs dry with a paper towel, then rub with the oil and place on the prepared pan.

3 Mix the salt, pepper, brown sugar, and garlic together in a small bowl and spread this mixture onto the chicken.

4 Transfer the sheet pan to the oven and bake for 30 to 35 minutes, until the chicken is crisp and golden brown and cooked through.

SUBSTITUTIONS

Chicken Thighs	4 pork loin chops	4 boneless, skinless chicken breasts
Garlic	2 teaspoons minced fresh ginger	2 teaspoons Sriracha

JALAPEÑO-BACON CHICKEN

My love for bacon-wrapped meats runs deep, and this recipe showcases why: It's savory, salty, and spicy—and all achieved with just three ingredients! Baking the chicken does two important things here: It allows the jalapeños to mellow, lending the dish just a subtle bite but lots of flavor, and it crisps up the bacon, making for a nice crunchy exterior. I use bone-in thighs because my kids like to grab these with their hands and devour them caveman-style. *Serves 4*

4 bone-in, skin-on chicken thighs

½ teaspoon kosher salt

¼ teaspoon coarsely ground black pepper

1 tablespoon vegetable oil

1 jalapeño, sliced into 12 rounds

8 slices bacon

1 Preheat the oven to 375°F/190°C.

2 Remove the skin from the chicken and make 3 (1-inch/2.5 cm) slits in the top of each thigh with a sharp knife.

3 Place the chicken on a sheet pan, season with the salt and pepper, and rub with the oil. Place 1 jalapeño slice into each slit.

4 Wrap 2 slices of bacon around each thigh, tucking the ends underneath the chicken.

5 Bake until the chicken is cooked through and the bacon is crispy, 25 to 30 minutes, depending on the size of the thighs.

SUBSTITUTIONS

Chicken Thighs	4 boneless, skinless chicken breasts	1 (2-pound/910 g) pork tenderloin
Jalapeño	3 cloves garlic, minced	¼ cup/55 g packed light brown sugar

BAKED CHICKEN WINGS

This is a perfect party dish. It's all the fun of chicken wings without the potential pitfalls: You don't run the risk of staining your shirt or burning your mouth. If you want to dress it up, serve the wings with a side of ranch dressing or marinara sauce.

Parmesan cheese is low in moisture, but when paired with the fat from the chicken wings, it creates a beautiful crust that simulates a more complicated breading. Lemon zest added at the end contributes brightness and a little zing. *Serves 4 or 5 as a main course, or 8 as an appetizer*

---

4 pounds/1.8 kg chicken wings

2 tablespoons olive oil

1 teaspoon kosher salt

½ teaspoon coarsely ground black pepper

¾ cup/70 g grated Parmesan cheese

Grated zest of 1 lemon

1 Preheat the oven to 400°F/205°C. Line a sheet pan with parchment paper or aluminum foil.

2 Pat the chicken wings dry with paper towels and place in a large bowl. Add the olive oil, salt, pepper, and ½ cup/50 g of the Parmesan cheese and toss well.

3 Turn the chicken out onto the prepared pan in a single layer. Bake for 30 to 35 minutes, until crispy and browned.

4 While the wings are still hot, toss with the lemon zest and the remaining ¼ cup/20 g Parmesan.

SUBSTITUTIONS

Parmesan Cheese	¼ cup/60 ml peanut butter, tossed with the chicken in Step 2	⅓ cup/80 ml Thai green curry paste, tossed with the chicken in Step 2	1 cup/170 g canned pineapple chunks, with ¼ cup/60 ml of their juice, tossed with the chicken in Step 2
Lemon Zest	¼ cup/60 ml low-sodium soy sauce	1 (13.5-ounce/ 400 ml) can coconut milk	no change to recipe

Classic Recipe
PERFECT ROAST CHICKEN

Everyone needs a fail-safe recipe for roast chicken. This one produces a chicken that is juicy, crispy on the outside, and perfectly cooked through—exactly what you want in a roast chicken. It's so good that I'm confident you'll never buy a rotisserie chicken again. Think of this recipe as just a template. Once you've got this method down, you can add whatever herbs, spices, and/or other flavors your heart desires.

HERE ARE THE BASICS:

▶ Salt your chicken. I salt mine pretty heavily, about 2 teaspoons kosher salt for a 4-pound/1.8 kg chicken. But this does not make for a salty chicken. Some of this salt will permeate the meat, but much of it will function to draw moisture out of the skin, giving it a perfect crispiness. If you need to scale back on the salt due to health concerns, you can achieve a crispy skin by carefully drying the skin with paper towels before cooking. (I stress "carefully," because a bunch of paper towels soaked with raw chicken juices is a good way to spread salmonella around the kitchen.) In addition to the salt,

I season the chicken with pepper. If you've cut back on the amount of salt, you might want to bump up the amount of pepper a bit.

▶ Don't add any additional liquids to the roasting pan. The salt you've added to the skin along with the fat that will render out of the bird while cooking will provide all the liquid you need. Adding liquid—water, broth, wine, etc.—would make for less crispy skin, increase the cooking time, and dry out the chicken. It's good to remember this as you start improvising with the recipe: Dry seasonings are good, added liquid is not.

▶ Once your chicken is in the oven, pretend there's a delicate soufflé in there and don't open the door. Every time you open the oven door, you let out a lot of heat, and it will take time for the oven to reach the correct temperature again. Not only does this increase the cooking time, you're also effectively lowering the cooking temperature by letting in cold air, which will make for soggy skin. So, once the chicken is in the oven, leave it alone—there's nothing to see in there!

Serves 4 to 5

1 (4- to 5-pound/
1.8 to 2.3 kg) chicken,
giblets discarded

1 to 2 tablespoons
unsalted butter,
softened/melted

2 teaspoons kosher
salt

½ teaspoon coarsely
ground black pepper

½ teaspoon dried
thyme

1 teaspoon onion
powder

1 Preheat the oven to 425°F/220°C.

2 Dry the chicken inside and out with paper towels. Rub the butter over the entire bird, then season inside and out with the salt, pepper, thyme, and onion powder.

3 Place the chicken in a roasting pan and roast for 15 minutes, then lower the heat to 375°F/190°C and cook for 40 to 45 minutes longer, until the center of the thigh reads 165°F/74°C on a meat thermometer. When the thigh is pierced with a knife, the juices should run clear. Loosely tent the chicken with foil and let rest for about 10 minutes before serving.

SUBSTITUTIONS

Thyme	½ teaspoon dried rosemary + grated zest and juice of 1 lemon
	1 teaspoon paprika + 1 teaspoon dried oregano
	½ teaspoon ground cumin + ½ teaspoon ground coriander
	3 cloves garlic, minced + grated zest and juice of 1 lemon
	1 apple, quartered (place in the chicken's cavity) + ½ teaspoon ground sage rubbed on chicken

SWEET-AND-SPICY TILAPIA

This sauce, one of my favorites, takes advantage of two items I always have in my pantry, Sriracha and honey. It spices up just about any dish you can imagine. One word of caution: Honey burns easily, as I learned the first time I made this fish—I added the honey-Sriracha sauce before the fish went into the oven and ended up with a kitchen full of smoke. Now I add the sauce just a few minutes before the end of cooking. That still gives it plenty of time to flavor the fish, but you don't run the risk of burning the sauce. *Serves 4*

1 tablespoon vegetable oil, plus (optional) more for coating the pan

4 (6-ounce/170 g) tilapia fillets

½ teaspoon kosher salt

⅛ teaspoon coarsely ground black pepper

¼ cup/60 ml honey

1 teaspoon Sriracha

1 Preheat the oven to 400°F/205°C. Coat a sheet pan with vegetable oil, or spray it with nonstick vegetable oil spray.

2 Rub the tilapia with 1 tablespoon oil, then season with the salt and pepper. Place on the prepared pan.

3 In a small bowl, mix the honey and Sriracha.

4 Bake the tilapia for 8 minutes. Spoon over the honey sauce and bake for an additional 3 minutes.

SUBSTITUTIONS

Tilapia	4 (6-ounce/170 g) salmon fillets	4 (6-ounce/170 g) cod fillets
Honey	¼ cup/60 ml sweet chili sauce	3 tablespoons light brown sugar
Sriracha	2 cloves garlic, minced	Grated zest of 1 lime

Classic Recipe
ROAST PORK LOIN

A roast pork loin is an impressive centerpiece for a dinner party. Pork loin is healthy, and with minimal prep, you have a very flavorful main course. Like the roast chicken recipe on page 62, think of this as a blank canvas; there are an almost infinite number of seasonings (and sides) you can pair with the pork to make an unforgettable meal. But first master the basic principles for a tender and perfectly cooked roast:

Start by buying a roast with a thick, even layer of fat. Pork is lean, like chicken breasts, but the fat will ensure the meat stays moist. Look for a roast with at least a ¼-inch/6 mm layer of fat; more is better. You will most likely be cutting this away when you eat it, so don't be afraid of a thick fat cap. If you're buying your pork prepackaged and wrapped in plastic, it can be hard to gauge the thickness. For that reason, I prefer to buy my roast (or really any cut of meat) from the meat counter, where I can get a good look at it.

It's in a market's best interest to sell you as large a piece of meat as they can, which is why it's common to see 6- to 7-pound/2.7 to 3.2 kg pork loin roasts, though about 3 pounds/1.4 kg is really ideal for feeding six people. If you have to buy a larger roast, don't worry—just cut it in half, wrap one half tightly in plastic, and freeze it (be sure to date it). I don't love cooking a larger pork roast than I expect to serve because the lean meat typically doesn't reheat all that well.

To give my pork an extra layer of protection, I coat it lightly with vegetable oil, about 3 tablespoons rubbed evenly over the roast. Then it's off to the oven. It's cooked at high heat for 60 to 75 minutes. Lower heat and a longer cooking time will leach out the moisture and yield a dry, tough piece of meat.

You can dress up this roast in any number of ways, but one easy way is to cut a crosshatch pattern in the top layer of fat. You just want to score the fat, not cut all the way through to the meat. Crosshatching does a number of beneficial things: It helps any seasonings you've added stay on top of the roast rather than sliding off; it results in better browning because there is more surface area exposed to the heat; and, finally, it makes for a very fancy-looking roast.

1 (3- to 4-pound/
1.4 to 1.8 kg) boneless
pork loin roast
(not tenderloin)

3 tablespoons
vegetable oil

4 cloves garlic, minced

½ teaspoon kosher
salt

½ teaspoon coarsely
ground black pepper

¼ teaspoon paprika

1 Preheat the oven to 375°F/190°C.

2 Place the pork in a roasting pan and rub it with the oil, making sure to coat it evenly. Massage the garlic into the fat cap.

3 Mix the salt, pepper, and paprika in a small bowl and rub this mixture all over the pork. Score the fat cap.

4 Roast the pork for 60 to 75 minutes, until it has reached an internal temperature of 150° to 160°F/65° to 70°C when tested with a meat thermometer. The top should be golden brown and the meat should have some springiness when gently pressed.

5 Remove the pork from the oven and let it rest for 5 minutes. Carve it in 3/4- to 1-inch/2 to 2.5 cm thick slices. If you're serving the roast for a buffet, your slices can be a bit thinner, about ¼ inch/6 mm.

ADDITIONAL FLAVORING OPTIONS

In place of the paprika and some or all of the garlic, try these seasonings:

¼ cup/60 ml honey + 3 cloves garlic, minced

2 tablespoons soy sauce + 2 tablespoons light brown sugar +
2 teaspoons sesame oil

3 cloves garlic, minced + ½ teaspoon dried oregano +
¼ teaspoon dried basil

1 tablespoon chopped fresh dill + grated zest of 1 lemon

½ teaspoon crushed fennel seeds + 2 tablespoons Dijon mustard

2 tablespoons chili powder + 3 tablespoons light brown sugar

½ cup/120 ml apple jelly + ½ teaspoon rubbed sage

BRUSSELS SPROUTS WITH BACON AND APRICOTS

Bacon and Brussels sprouts are basically best friends in our house. The apricots are a fun twist I discovered one Easter dinner when I realized we were out of the dried cranberries I usually pair with sprouts. The combination is now a family favorite, and I've never looked back. *Serves 4*

6 slices bacon, diced

2 pounds/910 kg Brussels sprouts

½ cup/64 g diced dried apricots

1 teaspoon kosher salt

¼ teaspoon coarsely ground black pepper

1 Put the bacon in a cast-iron skillet over medium heat and cook until the fat has rendered. Using a slotted spoon, remove the bacon, leaving the fat in the pan, and set aside. Set the pan aside for now.

2 Trim and halve the Brussels sprouts. Add them to a large microwave-safe bowl and cover with a wet paper towel. Microwave on high for 5 to 6 minutes.

3 Remove the Brussels sprouts from the bowl and pat them dry with a paper towel. Return the skillet to medium heat, add the Brussels sprouts, and cook until crispy, 5 to 7 minutes.

4 Meanwhile, add the apricots to a small bowl, cover with hot water, and microwave for 1 minute.

5 Drain the apricots, add to the skillet, and stir well. Return the bacon to the pan and give the whole thing another quick stir, then serve.

ASPARAGUS WITH LEMON AND RICOTTA

This vegetable side dish is quick enough to serve with a rotisserie chicken on a weeknight but special enough for a holiday meal. Ricotta is an unsung hero among cheeses, and it shines with lemon. This recipe employs one of my favorite kitchen hacks: cooking vegetables in the microwave before finishing them on the stovetop; it makes dinnertime a breeze. *Serves 4 to 6*

---

1 bunch asparagus
(about 2 pounds/
910 g)

2 tablespoons extra-
virgin olive oil

Kosher salt

¼ teaspoon coarsely
ground black pepper

Grated zest and juice
of 1 lemon (about
3 tablespoons juice)

½ cup/125 g
whole-milk ricotta

1 Trim the asparagus and cut into 2-inch/5 cm pieces. Place in a microwave-safe bowl, cover with a wet paper towel, and microwave on high for 3 minutes.

2 Heat the oil in a large skillet over high heat. Once the oil is hot, add the asparagus, ½ teaspoon salt, and the pepper and cook, stirring occasionally, for 3 to 4 minutes. Add the lemon juice and stir.

3 Mix the ricotta, lemon zest, and salt to taste in a small bowl. Serve alongside the asparagus.

GARLICKY BROCCOLI AND CAULIFLOWER

Steaming vegetables is an easy and healthy way to prepare them, but if overcooked, they can quickly lose their texture and flavor. Mushy vegetables paired with mystery sauces makes them doubly unappealing. Instead, try crisping up barely steamed vegetables in a skillet with butter and garlic, as I do here. *Serves 4*

3 cups/275 g broccoli florets

3 cups/400 g cauliflower florets

1 teaspoon kosher salt

¼ teaspoon coarsely ground black pepper

3 tablespoons unsalted butter

3 cloves garlic, minced

1 Put the broccoli and cauliflower in a large skillet with a lid set over medium heat, add ½ cup/120 ml water, cover, and steam for 5 minutes.

2 Remove the lid and allow the remaining water to cook off for a minute or two.

3 Add the salt, pepper, and 2 tablespoons of the butter to the skillet. Once the butter has melted, toss the broccoli and cauliflower to coat and then cook for 2 to 3 minutes, until the edges start to brown.

4 Add the minced garlic, along with the remaining 1 tablespoon butter, and allow the garlic to bloom (you'll begin to smell it), then give the vegetables a good stir.

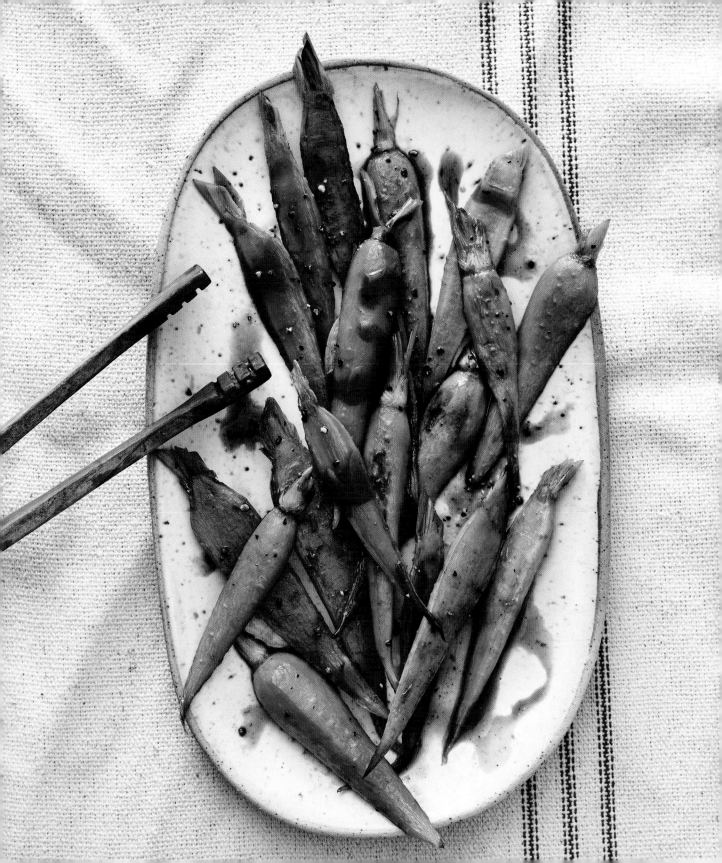

BALSAMIC-BROWN SUGAR CARROTS

Carrots don't seem like they would need a gentle hand in the kitchen; they're so tough, they withstand weeks in the crisper drawer without showing a blemish. But somehow, expose them to heat and they turn to mush. Literally. Add a honey glaze, which so many people feel inclined to do, and they're a sweet, sticky mush. However, if treated with the care they deserve, cooked carrots can be a great side. Here I slice them, steam them until just barely tender, and then coat them in a balsamic vinegar reduction. The vinegar cuts the sweetness of the brown sugar and adds depth. A side dish worthy of your next holiday table. *Serves 4 to 6*

---

5 medium carrots, halved lengthwise

1 tablespoon olive oil

¼ teaspoon kosher salt

⅛ teaspoon coarsely ground black pepper

2 tablespoons balsamic vinegar

2 tablespoons light brown sugar

1 Add ¼ cup/60 ml water to a medium saucepan with a tight-fitting lid and set over medium-high heat. Add the carrots, cover, and steam for 4 to 5 minutes. Drain the carrots.

2 Return the pan to medium-high heat and allow it to dry for 10 seconds. Add the oil, carrots, salt, and pepper and cook for 1 minute, stirring occasionally.

3 Add the balsamic vinegar and brown sugar to the pan and stir well to combine. Let the carrots simmer for about 2 minutes, stirring occasionally, until they are well coated with the glaze.

PERFECT PILAF

Growing up in an Armenian household, we never ate plain white rice; instead, it was always seasoned like this. The buttery texture of the rice and the toasted noodles make the dish feel fancy and rich, but it only takes a few more minutes than your basic boiled rice. Play around with the type of rice you use: Basmati will add a more Middle Eastern quality and it will be simultaneously fluffier and a bit drier. Standard long-grain rice, like Uncle Ben's, holds more moisture. This is lovely with the Citrus Salmon (page 46) or Greek Lemon Chicken (page 113). *Serves 4*

---

4 ounces/115 g vermicelli noodles (coiled nests)

4 tablespoons/55 g unsalted butter

2 cups/475 ml chicken broth

½ teaspoon kosher salt

⅛ teaspoon coarsely ground black pepper

1 cup/185 g long-grain white rice

1 Break the vermicelli into small pieces (about ½ inch/13 mm; you'll have about ½ cup) and place in a large pot with a tight-fitting lid.

2 Add the butter to the pot and melt it over medium heat, stirring, then continue stirring and cooking the vermicelli until golden brown, 4 to 5 minutes.

3 Add the chicken broth, salt, pepper, and rice to the pot and stir well. Bring the broth to a boil, cover, reduce the heat to a simmer, and cook the rice for 20 minutes.

4 Let the rice sit off the heat for 5 minutes before removing the lid and fluffing it with a fork.

EASY MEXICAN RICE

Salsa adds all the flavor you need to elevate this rice from a bland starch to an exciting side dish. I love using jarred salsas of all varieties, but a fresh pico de gallo will work equally well. You can use this same strategy with other sides—with a little doctoring, a simple can of refried beans can be transformed into something delicious. Here toasting the rice first helps prevent it from sticking together. This is the perfect side for the Cuban Pork (page 158). *Serves 4*

2 tablespoons vegetable oil

1½ cups/275 g long-grain white rice

2 cups/475 ml chicken broth

1 cup/235 ml jarred salsa

½ teaspoon kosher salt

¼ teaspoon coarsely ground black pepper

1 Heat the oil in a Dutch oven over medium-high heat. Add the rice and stir until translucent, 3 to 4 minutes.

2 Add the chicken broth, salsa, salt, and pepper and stir well. Bring to a boil, cover, reduce the heat to a simmer, and cook for 20 minutes.

3 Let the rice sit off the heat for 5 minutes. Remove the lid and fluff the rice with a fork before serving.

PARMESAN-BACON POTATOES

Grated Parmesan cheese acts as a flavorful coating for these potatoes, which get a double dose of crispiness from the bacon. This dish is ideal alongside eggs for a weekend brunch. It's also great served with grilled meats for a summer cookout.

Serves 4

2 pounds/910 g Yukon Gold potatoes, scrubbed and cut into 1-inch/2.5 cm chunks

½ teaspoon kosher salt

¼ teaspoon coarsely ground black pepper

2 tablespoons vegetable oil

6 slices bacon, roughly chopped

½ cup/50 g grated Parmesan cheese

1 Preheat the oven to 400°F/205°C. Line a sheet pan with parchment paper.

2 Add the potatoes, salt, pepper, vegetable oil, chopped bacon, and half of the Parmesan cheese to a large bowl and toss well.

3 Transfer the potatoes to the lined sheet pan, arranging them in a single layer, and bake for 20 minutes.

4 Give the potatoes a stir, sprinkle with the remaining Parmesan, and bake for an additional 15 minutes, or until crispy and browned.

CHAPTER TWO

5

Ingredient

DINNERS

SKILLET CAESAR PASTA

Watching Wolfgang Puck in the early days of food television was a defining pastime for me as a young adult. His reassuring, encouraging, and enthusiastic approach to cooking was captivating. And back in those days, all the cooking was happening in real time, so when he made a sauce or panfried fish, I would follow along to see the transformations taking place.

One of my all-time favorite recipes from those old Wolfgang Puck shows was a Caesar dressing. I furiously scribbled down notes from that show and kept that piece of paper for many years, pulling it out anytime I wanted to make the zesty sauce. I use the dressing on everything from cold pasta salad to leafy green salads, in baked pasta casseroles, and, here, in a quick skillet pasta. I mix the dressing with cooked spaghetti and add a little more Parmesan cheese and a bit of lemon zest. You can add broiled chicken breast if you're looking for protein, and if you want a little more texture and bite, add some cherry or grape tomatoes. Eat it immediately, or let it cool to room temperature and pack it for a picnic. *Serves 6*

¼ teaspoon kosher salt, plus more for the pasta cooking water

1 pound/455 g thin spaghetti

1 teaspoon Worcestershire sauce

1 cup/100 g grated Parmesan cheese (use the large holes of a box grater)

Grated zest and juice of 1 large lemon (¼ cup/60 ml juice)

¼ cup/60 ml olive oil

¼ cup/60 ml vegetable oil

2 cloves garlic

¼ teaspoon coarsely ground black pepper

1 Bring a large pot of heavily salted water to a boil. Add the pasta and cook for 1 minute shy of the package directions. Drain.

2 Meanwhile, make the Caesar dressing: Add the Worcestershire sauce, half the Parmesan cheese, the lemon juice, olive oil, vegetable oil, garlic, salt, and pepper to a food processor and pulse for 30 seconds, or until smooth.

3 Add the Caesar dressing to a large skillet and heat over medium heat for 30 seconds, then add the pasta and toss to coat.

4 Stir in the remaining Parmesan cheese and the lemon zest and serve.

SUBSTITUTIONS

Spaghetti	4 boneless, skinless chicken breasts, broiled then sliced	1 head Romaine lettuce, chopped
Vegetable Oil	½ cup/120 ml mayonnaise	no change to recipe

VEGETABLE GREEN CURRY

This curry is a perfect example of cooking wholesome, satisfying food almost entirely from pantry staples. It relies on two easy-to-find ingredients—jarred or canned curry paste and coconut milk—and can be kept simple and vegetarian, or decked out with shrimp or chicken, chiles, thai basil, or more vegetables—you name it. It's flavorful but not overcomplicated, and because it's not a prepackaged sauce, you can control the spiciness. One note about fresh versus frozen broccoli: Fresh broccoli is infinitely better here because it will retain some crunch; if you use the frozen variety, you will end up with a mushy texture. Serve this over rice for a complete meal. *Serves 4*

4 cups/365 g broccoli florets

3 carrots, peeled and thinly sliced on the bias (about ¼ inch/ 6 mm thick)

2 zucchini, cut lengthwise in half and sliced about ¼ inch/ 6 mm thick

¼ teaspoon kosher salt

Pinch of coarsely ground black pepper

2 tablespoons vegetable oil

2 tablespoons Thai green curry paste

1 (13.5-ounce/400 ml) can full-fat coconut milk

1 Add 1 cup/235 ml water to a large pot with a tight-fitting lid and bring to a boil, then add the broccoli and carrots, cover, and steam for 2 minutes.

2 Remove the lid and let the water cook off completely—the pot should be completely dry. Add the zucchini, salt, pepper, and oil, toss to coat the vegetables, and cook for 4 to 5 minutes to brown the vegetables slightly.

3 Add the curry paste and stir well, then slowly pour in the coconut milk and mix thoroughly. Cook the curry for 3 more minutes. Serve over rice.

SUBSTITUTIONS

Broccoli	1 (16-ounce/455 g) bag stir-fry veggies, fresh or frozen	no change to recipe
Carrots	1 teaspoon minced ginger, added in Step 2	2 pounds/910 g (13–15 count) shrimp, peeled and deveined, added in Step 3
Zucchini	3 cloves garlic, minced, added in Step 2	3 cloves garlic, minced, added in Step 2
Thai Green Curry Paste	½ cup/120 ml teriyaki sauce, added in Step 3	½ cup/120 ml hoisin sauce, added in Step 3
Coconut Milk	2 teaspoons sesame oil, added in Step 3	2 teaspoons sesame oil, added in Step 3

CREAMY TOMATO SALMON

This is a luxurious and, as its name promises, creamy sauce. Tomato paste is a secret ingredient when you want to add a punch of tomato flavor without the liquid of canned or fresh tomatoes, which can yield a watery sauce. Sun-dried tomatoes bring additional concentrated tomato flavor, as well as some welcome texture. A bit of heavy cream gives the sauce its richness and smooth consistency.

This dish comes together quickly, so have all your ingredients close by and at the ready. *Serves 4*

4 (6-ounce/170 g) salmon fillets, skin on

½ teaspoon kosher salt

¼ teaspoon coarsely ground black pepper

2 tablespoons unsalted butter

¼ cup/43 g chopped sun-dried tomatoes (if oil-packed, drain them before using)

2 cloves garlic, minced

2 tablespoons tomato paste

½ cup/120 ml heavy cream

1 Season the salmon with the salt and pepper.

2 Heat a large skillet over medium-high heat, then add the butter. Once it has melted, add the salmon skin side down and cook for 4 minutes. Flip the salmon and cook for another 3 minutes, then transfer to a plate.

3 Add the sun-dried tomatoes and garlic to the pan and cook for 30 seconds. Whisk in the tomato paste and heavy cream and cook for 3 to 4 minutes, until the sauce has thickened.

4 Return the salmon to the pan, spoon the sauce over the top, and serve immediately.

SUBSTITUTIONS

Sun-dried Tomatoes	1 cup/155 g frozen spinach (thawed and drained well)	4 ounces/115 g jarred or canned artichoke hearts, drained and chopped
Tomato Paste	2 tablespoons all-purpose flour, to coat the salmon before cooking	¼ cup/25 g grated Parmesan cheese

CILANTRO-LIME SHRIMP

This quick stir-fry is flavor-packed. It has sweetness, some acidity, and smokiness from the cumin. It'll have every one of your senses firing! It is guaranteed to snap you out of a midweek cooking rut. *Serves 6*

2 tablespoons
vegetable oil

2 pounds/910 g
(13–15 count) shrimp,
peeled, deveined, and
tails removed

½ teaspoon kosher
salt

1 teaspoon cumin
seeds

¼ cup/10 g minced
fresh cilantro

2 tablespoons honey

Grated zest and
juice of 1 lime (about
2 tablespoons juice)

1 Heat the oil in a large skillet over high heat. When the oil is hot, add the shrimp and cook for 1 minute on each side.

2 Add the salt, cumin, and cilantro, stir, and cook for 30 seconds more.

3 Remove the pan from the heat, add the honey, and the lime zest and juice, and stir until the honey is warmed and the sauce coats the shrimp. Serve immediately.

SUBSTITUTIONS

Shrimp	3 boneless, skinless chicken breasts, thinly sliced	4 (¾-inch-/2 cm thick) boneless pork loin chops
Honey	¼ cup/55 g packed light brown sugar	3 tablespoons maple syrup
Lime (zest and juice)	no change to recipe	2 tablespoons low-sodium soy sauce

LEMON-PARMESAN CHICKEN

Chicken Parm is widely loved, but for as many people who crave this classic, just as many tell me they don't feel great after eating it. The acidity and heaviness of the sauce is usually the culprit. I wanted to keep what makes Chicken Parm great—crispy chicken, creamy cheese—but give it a brighter flavor. The answer was lemon juice and zest. You can add a few splashes of white wine to the sauce when it's cooking for a more adult taste. And, as a bonus, it's all done in one skillet, making it a cinch to clean up.

This is delicious served with polenta, pasta, garlic mashed potatoes, or roasted sweet potatoes. *Serves 4*

2 boneless, skinless chicken breasts

½ teaspoon kosher salt

¼ teaspoon coarsely ground black pepper

2 large eggs

Grated zest and juice of 1 large lemon (¼ cup/60 ml juice)

1½ cups/120 g panko (Japanese bread crumbs)

⅓ cup/30 g grated Parmesan cheese

2 tablespoons olive oil

1 Lay the chicken breasts on a cutting board and slice each one horizontally in half so you have 4 thin cutlets. Season them with the salt and pepper.

2 Set up your breading station: Crack the eggs into a medium bowl and lightly beat them, then add the lemon juice. Mix the panko with half the Parmesan in a second medium bowl.

3 Working with one piece of chicken at a time, add to the egg mixture and turn to coat well, then press it into the panko mixture, turning once, until evenly covered. Transfer the breaded chicken breasts to a sheet pan and let sit for 5 minutes.

4 Heat 1 tablespoon of the oil in a large skillet over medium heat. When the oil is hot, add 2 of the chicken cutlets. Cook, turning once, for 4 to 5 minutes on each side, until golden brown and cooked through. Transfer to a plate, then add the remaining tablespoon of oil to the pan and repeat with the remaining 2 cutlets.

5 While the chicken is cooking, add the remaining Parmesan cheese and the lemon zest to a small bowl and mix well.

6 Serve the chicken with the lemon zest–Parmesan mixture sprinkled over it.

SUBSTITUTIONS

Chicken Breasts	4 (6-ounce/170 g) boneless pork loin chops	4 (6-ounce/170 g) salmon fillets	2 pounds/910 g (13–15 count) shrimp, peeled and deveined
Panko	1 cup/100 g bread crumbs	no change to recipe	no change to recipe
Lemon (zest and juice)	no change to recipe	1 teaspoon Sriracha	no change to recipe

GARLICKY MEATBALLS

It's always been important to me to raise my kids with adventurous palates. But with chicken on the docket so many nights of the week, I was beginning to worry it was becoming the only protein they would happily eat. Enter garlicky pork meatballs. Meatballs are fun to eat, and the shape is so familiar to kids. They are also a great thing to introduce to babies and toddlers who are just learning to feed themselves. And you can substitute whatever ground meat you'd like: chicken, beef, even lamb. These can be used in a variety of dishes; try them over rice, in lettuce cups, or in banh mi sandwiches. One important note: Overhandling (rolling and rerolling) ground meat will make for tough and less juicy meatballs, so roll them once and then leave them alone. *Serves 4; makes approximately 16 meatballs*

1 pound/455 g ground pork, thoroughly chilled

½ teaspoon kosher salt

⅓ teaspoon coarsely ground black pepper

2 cloves garlic, minced

½ cup/40 g panko (Japanese bread crumbs)

Grated zest and juice of 1 lime (about 2 tablespoons)

½ cup/120 ml plum sauce

2 tablespoons vegetable oil

1 In a large bowl, mix together the pork, salt, pepper, garlic, panko, lime zest and juice, and 1 tablespoon of the plum sauce. Roll the mixture into 1-inch/2.5 cm balls, being careful not to overhandle the meat. You should have about 16 meatballs.

2 Add the vegetable oil to a large skillet set over medium-high heat. Once the oil is hot add the meatballs to the pan, working in two batches, and sear, turning occasionally, until browned on all sides, 6 to 8 minutes; transfer the first batch of meatballs to a plate with a slotted spoon. Cook the remaining meatballs.

3 Return all the meatballs to the pan, add the remaining plum sauce, and toss to coat. Serve.

SUBSTITUTIONS

Ground Pork	1 pound/455 g ground chicken (not extra-lean)	1 pound/455 g ground turkey (not extra-lean)	1 pound/455 g lean (85/15) ground beef
Panko	⅓ cup/35 g bread crumbs	⅓ cup/30 g finely crushed saltines	no change to recipe
Plum Sauce	½ cup/120 ml sweet chili sauce	½ cup/120 ml hoisin sauce	no change to recipe

STEAK-AND-POTATO HASH

Breakfast for dinner is a favorite in my house, and this dish is easy and incredibly satisfying. Hash can often end up mushy and with muddled flavors. I've intentionally kept this recipe bare bones—think of it like a mini tutorial for making the best possible hash. Once you've got the technique down, you have a blank canvas for adding whatever other seasonings and flavorings you like.

First things first, start with the right potatoes. Yukon Golds have a delicious buttery flavor and flesh that holds their shape and won't get dry or mealy. They also have a thin skin, so you don't need to peel them. (Save your russets for Garlic-Cheddar Mashed Potatoes, page 185.) Next, in order to get a crispy, not mushy, hash restrain yourself from stirring it too much. Add your potatoes, give them a quick stir, and then allow them to sear. Following these two guidelines, you'll be on your way to a better hash. *Serves 6*

2 pounds/910 g Yukon Gold potatoes, scrubbed and cut into 1-inch/2.5 cm cubes

2 boneless rib-eye steaks (about 1 pound/455 g each)

1 teaspoon kosher salt

½ teaspoon coarsely ground black pepper

4 tablespoons/55 g unsalted butter

2 tablespoons vegetable oil

1 yellow onion, roughly chopped

1 red bell pepper, cored, seeded, and cut into 1-inch/2.5 cm squares

2 cloves garlic, minced

1 Put the potatoes in a large pot of salted water, bring to a boil, and cook for approximately 12 minutes, until you can easily pierce the potatoes with a fork. Drain and spread out on a sheet pan to dry thoroughly.

2 Season the steak with the salt and black pepper.

3 Heat a large cast-iron or other heavy skillet over medium heat and add 2 tablespoons of the butter and the vegetable oil. Once the butter has melted and the fat is hot, add the steaks to the pan and sear on each side for 5 minutes. Remove the steaks from the pan and let rest while you cook the vegetables.

4 Add the potatoes, making sure they are completely dry, the onion, and bell pepper to the pan, along with the remaining 2 tablespoons butter. Let the vegetables cook for 3 to 5 minutes, until the potatoes have a nice, crispy exterior, then add the garlic, stir, and cook for another 3 minutes.

5 Meanwhile, cut the steak into 1-inch/2.5 cm cubes. Add the steak back to the pan, turn the heat up to medium-high, and cook the steak with the vegetables for 5 minutes. Serve.

SUBSTITUTIONS

Yukon Gold Potatoes	2 pounds/910 g russet potatoes	2 pounds/910 g sweet potatoes
Rib-eye Steaks	2 pounds/455 g flank steak	no change to recipe
Onion	1 red onion, roughly chopped	4 slices bacon, chopped
Red Bell Pepper	½ teaspoon paprika	8 ounces/225 g Brussels sprouts, shaved

ASPARAGUS-STUFFED CHICKEN BREASTS

These compact little bundles make a fancy-looking dish that is surprisingly easy to prepare. If you buy stuffed chicken breasts at the deli counter, they will cost more than if you make them at home, so it makes sense to put them together yourself with a few inexpensive ingredients. Pounding the breasts with a mallet to flatten them can make for a tough, less juicy piece of meat, so I butterfly them instead. Choose a high-quality thinly sliced ham, or spring for its higher-end cousins, prosciutto or pancetta. *Serves 4*

4 boneless, skinless chicken breasts

¼ teaspoon kosher salt

¼ teaspoon coarsely ground black pepper

3 tablespoons olive oil

½ cup/50 g grated Parmesan cheese

2 cloves garlic, minced

12 spears asparagus, trimmed

4 slices ham

1 Butterfly each chicken breast by slicing it horizontally almost in half, being careful not to slice all the way through, and open it like a book. Lay the chicken out on your work surface, cut side up.

2 Sprinkle the chicken with the salt, pepper, 1 tablespoon of the olive oil, half of the Parmesan cheese, and half of the minced garlic.

3 Place 3 spears of asparagus on each slice of ham and top with the remaining Parmesan cheese and garlic. Wrap the edges of each slice of ham around the asparagus to make a flattened bundle (with the asparagus in a single layer instead of in a bunch) and place one packet inside each chicken breast. If your chicken bundles don't stay closed, you can secure them with toothpicks.

4 Heat the remaining 2 tablespoons olive oil in a large skillet over medium-low heat. Once the oil is hot, add the chicken and cook, turning once, for 7 to 8 minutes on each side, until the chicken is cooked all the way through. If the chicken is not browned when it is done, raise the heat and cook just long enough to brown it on the outside.

SUBSTITUTIONS

Chicken Breasts	4 (¾-inch/2 cm thick) boneless pork loin chops
Parmesan Cheese	4 slices provolone cheese
Garlic	1 tablespoon chopped fresh thyme
Asparagus	1 Fuji apple, halved, cored, and thinly sliced
Ham	8 slices bacon

SLOW-COOKER STUFFED PEPPERS

Despite their enduring popularity, stuffed peppers are often both undercooked and underseasoned. The timing can be confounding—to get a perfectly cooked pepper, you run the risk of winding up with mushy rice or scorched bottoms. The answer is, as it is with many of life's questions (at least of the kitchen variety), the slow cooker. The gentle heat ensures that everything is cooked through and not torched.

And as for the problem of blandness, I turn to Italian seasoning, which adds a lot of flavor without requiring a lot of separate ingredients. This is a complete vegetarian main course, though of course you can "beef it up" with ground beef, chicken, or lamb.

Serves 6

¾ cup/140 g long-grain white rice

2 tablespoons olive oil

1 yellow onion, diced

2 cups/475 ml tomato sauce

½ teaspoon kosher salt

¼ teaspoon coarsely ground black pepper

1 teaspoon Italian seasoning

6 bell peppers, green or red

1 To parcook the rice, place it in a saucepan with 2 cups/475 ml water, bring to a boil, and boil for 8 minutes. Drain and set aside.

2 Add the olive oil to a large skillet and heat over medium-high heat. Once the oil is hot, add the onion and cook until translucent, 5 to 7 minutes.

3 Add the tomato sauce, salt, pepper, Italian seasoning, and rice and mix well. Remove from the heat.

4 Cut the tops off the peppers, ½ inch/13 mm below the stems, and discard. Remove the seeds and membranes. Add about ½ cup/120 ml of the filling to each pepper. Place the stuffed peppers in the slow cooker and add 1 cup/235 ml water.

5 Cook on low for 6 hours, or until the rice is tender.

SUBSTITUTIONS

White Rice	½ cup/85 g quinoa, rinsed and parcooked	2 cups/214 g uncooked cauliflower rice
Bell Peppers	3 medium zucchini, halved lengthwise and seeds scooped out	6 beefsteak tomatoes, cored, tops removed, and seeds scooped out

BACON-BROWN SUGAR "ROTISSERIE" CHICKEN

I call this rotisserie chicken because it has the same crispy skin you find on the store-bought version. Bacon and brown sugar are one of the world's great flavor combinations. For this recipe, I make a coil of aluminum foil for the chicken to sit on in the slow cooker to keep it out of the fat that will render as it cooks. I put the onions on top of that before I add the chicken so they will soak up all of that sweet smoky flavor. The onions become almost melted and make a fantastic side dish for the chicken. If you want the bacon to get crispy, put a clean dish towel under the slow-cooker lid to absorb the condensation from the steam and keep it from dripping back onto the chicken.

If you don't have a slow cooker, this can definitely be done in the oven. Cook it at 425°F/220°C for 15 minutes, then reduce the heat to 375°F/190°C and cook for another 40 to 45 minutes. You may need to loosely tent the chicken with foil if you see it browning too much. Enjoy, and you're welcome! *Serves 4*

2 yellow onions, cut into wedges

½ teaspoon kosher salt

¼ teaspoon coarsely ground black pepper

⅓ cup/75 g packed light brown sugar

2 tablespoons minced garlic

1 (4- to 5-pound/ 1.8 to 2.3 kg) chicken

10 slices bacon

1 Place the onions in the bottom of the slow cooker.

2 Mix the salt, pepper, brown sugar, and garlic in a small bowl. Rub this mixture all over the chicken, massaging it into the skin. Drape the chicken with the bacon, letting it wrap around the breasts.

3 Scrunch or roll a large sheet of aluminum foil into a rope, then coil this into a shape that fits snugly at the bottom of your slow cooker. Place the chicken on top of the coil and cook on low for 8 hours. If you find the chicken is not deeply caramelized after this time, it may be that your slow cooker runs a little cool. In that case, transfer the chicken to a sheet pan and cook under a preheated broiler for a minute or two while watching it like a hawk and removing it before the garlic starts to burn. Carve the chicken and serve with the onions.

SUBSTITUTIONS

Onions	2 pounds/910 g carrots, cut into 2-inch/5 cm chunks	no change to recipe
Chicken	1 (6-pound/2.7 kg) bone-in pork shoulder roast	1 (5-pound/2.3 kg) chuck roast

APPLE CIDER PORK

Pork is a great white-meat alternative to chicken, and apples and pork are a delicious and timeless combination. Together they create a perfectly balanced roast, savory and filling, with a touch of sweetness and not much heaviness. The apple comes in two forms—chunks of whole apples and apple cider—both of which cut through the fattiness of the pork. I leave the peel on the apples because the pectin it contains adds a bit of body to the sauce and prevents the apples from disintegrating when cooked. The onion, thyme, and cider make this comforting dish especially appropriate for the holidays. However, as we need easy and satisfying food all year round, swapping citrus for the apple easily turns this into a bright springtime dish.

If you don't have apple cider, you can add a tablespoon or so of applesauce to apple juice, but the resulting sauce might lack some of the depth. *Serves 12*

---

1 (5-pound/
2.3 kg) boneless
pork shoulder
(6 pounds/2.7 kg
if bone-in)

1 teaspoon kosher salt

½ teaspoon coarsely
ground black pepper

1 tablespoon
vegetable oil

2 yellow onions,
cut into 2-inch/5 cm
wedges

2 cups/475 ml apple
cider

2 tart apples (I like
Granny Smith), cored
and cut into 2-inch/
5 cm cubes

2 sprigs fresh thyme
or 1 teaspoon dried
thyme

1 Preheat the oven to 325°F/165°C.

2 Season the pork with the salt and pepper.

3 Heat the oil in a large Dutch oven over medium-high heat. Once the oil is hot, add the pork and brown well on all sides, 3 to 4 minutes per side.

4 Remove the pork and add the onion wedges to the pot. Cook for a few minutes, letting them get a little color but being careful not to let them burn.

5 Return the pork to the pot, placing it on the bed of onions. Add the cider and 1 cup/235 ml water and bring to a simmer, then wedge the apple pieces under the meat among the onions. Toss in the thyme.

6 Cover and transfer to the oven. Cook for 3 hours, or until the meat is fork-tender, shreds easily, and is a deep brown color; the apples will have caramelized.

SUBSTITUTIONS

Pork Shoulder	6 turkey thighs (cook for 2½ to 3 hours)	no change to recipe
Thyme	½ teaspoon ground cinnamon	½ teaspoon dried sage

RED WINE BEEF RAGÙ

This tastes like an all-day intensive Sunday roast, but the truth is it comes together in a flash. It's a special dish owing to the natural complexity the wine brings, the hint of sweetness from the balsamic vinegar, and the tang and acidity of the tomatoes. In other words, it's a perfectly balanced and rich sauce. Serve over rigatoni or mashed potatoes.

Serves 6

1 (4-pound/1.8 kg) chuck roast

2 teaspoons kosher salt

½ teaspoon coarsely ground black pepper

2 tablespoons olive oil

2 cups/475 ml red wine

1 (28-ounce/795 g) can diced tomatoes

¼ cup/60 ml balsamic vinegar

3 cloves garlic, minced

NOTE: *Alternatively, you can cook this, covered, in the oven for 3 hours at 325°F/165°C.*

1 Season the beef with the salt and pepper.

2 Heat the oil in a Dutch oven over medium-high heat. Once the oil is hot, sear the beef on all sides until deeply browned, 5 to 6 minutes per side.

3 Transfer the beef to a slow cooker and add the wine, tomatoes, vinegar, and garlic. Cook on low for 8 hours, or until it has a nice exterior crust and there is no resistance when the beef is pricked with a fork.

4 Using two forks, pull apart the beef into small chunks. Give it a good stir so the pieces of beef are well coated in sauce.

SUBSTITUTIONS

Chuck Roast	3 pounds/1.4 kg short ribs	2 pounds/910 g lean (85/15) ground beef
Canned Tomatoes	1 (28-ounce/795 g) can stewed tomatoes	no change to recipe

GINGER-SOY SALMON

If you're a fan of teriyaki anything, you'll love this. It's a reliable Asian-inspired dish that comes together quickly. While you might be tempted to use sesame oil in place of the vegetable oil, I'd caution that with so many strong flavors at play, the sesame runs the risk of being too much. And speaking of strong flavors, this dish relies on the pungency of fresh ginger and garlic. Using dried spices would result in a flat sauce.

Serves 4

¼ cup/60 ml low-sodium soy sauce

3 tablespoons honey

1 teaspoon minced fresh ginger

2 cloves garlic, minced

4 (6-ounce/170 g) salmon fillets, skin-on

2 tablespoons vegetable oil

¼ teaspoon kosher salt

Pinch of coarsely ground black pepper

1 In a small bowl, mix together the soy sauce, honey, ginger, and garlic.

2 Place the salmon in a shallow baking dish and coat with the soy-ginger mixture. Allow the salmon to marinate for 15 minutes at room temperature.

3 Transfer the salmon to a sheet pan, skin side down. Reserve the marinade.

4 Turn the oven to broil and position an oven rack 8 inches/20 cm from the heating element. Cook the salmon on high for 6 to 8 minutes.

5 Pour the marinade into a small saucepan and bring to a boil over medium heat. Remove from the heat and spoon over the cooked salmon.

SUBSTITUTIONS

Honey	3 tablespoons maple syrup	¼ cup/55 g packed light brown sugar	no change to recipe
Ginger	1 teaspoon Sriracha	no change to recipe	no change to recipe
Garlic	1 tablespoon ginger-garlic paste	no change to recipe	no change to recipe
Salmon	4 (6-ounce/170 g) cod fillets, skin on	4 boneless, skinless chicken breasts	4 pork loin chops (totaling 3½ to 4 pounds/1.6 to 1.8 kg)

CRISPY GARLIC SHRIMP

Although this shrimp isn't fried, it has an addictive and satisfying crunch—making it a perfect appetizer for parties. Many people are intimidated by the idea of quick high-heat cooking in a skillet or wok, especially with a delicate ingredient like shrimp. Baking the shrimp makes it a low- (or no!) stress alternative. *Serves 6 as a main course, or 8 as an appetizer*

2 pounds/910 g
(13–15 count) shrimp,
peeled and deveined

4 tablespoons/55 g
unsalted butter, melted

Grated zest of
1 lemon, plus 1 lemon,
cut into wedges,
for serving

4 cloves garlic, minced

½ cup/50 g grated
Parmesan cheese

1½ cups/120 g panko
(Japanese bread
crumbs)

1 Preheat the oven to 400°F/205°C.

2 In a medium bowl, toss the shrimp with the melted butter.

3 In a second medium bowl, mix the lemon zest, garlic, Parmesan, and panko. Working with one shrimp at a time, press the shrimp into the panko mixture to coat evenly on both sides and transfer to a sheet pan.

4 Bake the shrimp for 12 to 15 minutes; they should be lightly browned and crispy.

5 Serve the lemon wedges alongside the shrimp.

SUBSTITUTIONS

Shrimp	4 (6-ounce/170 g) salmon fillets, skinless	2 boneless, skinless chicken breasts, butterflied (see Asparagus-Stuffed Chicken Breasts, page 96, for instructions)
Panko	1 cup/90 g Ritz cracker crumbs	1 cup/100 g bread crumbs

CRANBERRY-GOAT CHEESE CHICKEN

Goat cheese and dried cranberries are a time-tested combination in salads and on cheese plates, but they don't seem to make it into cooked dishes very often. I had a hunch they would be just as delicious stuffed into chicken breasts and baked and, happily, I was right. Goat cheese packs a punch, so a little goes a long way; same with the cranberries, which are tart and tangy. Bone-in, skin-on chicken breasts are your best bet here. When these are stuffed and ready to cook, I lean the breasts against each other upright in the pan; this protects the thinner part of the breasts from overcooking and ensures that the thicker side and the stuffing are cooked through. *Serves 4*

4 bone-in, skin-on chicken breasts

½ teaspoon kosher salt

¼ teaspoon coarsely ground black pepper

¼ cup/60 ml balsamic vinegar

3 cloves garlic, minced

¼ cup/30 g goat cheese

¼ cup/35 g dried cranberries

1 Preheat the oven to 375°F/190°C.

2 Cut a slit down the length of the thicker side of each chicken breast as deep as you can go without cutting the breast in half. Season the chicken inside and out with the salt, pepper, and balsamic vinegar.

3 In a small bowl, mash together the garlic, goat cheese, and cranberries.

4 Stuff the goat cheese mixture into the chicken breasts, making sure to push the mixture deep into each pocket so it won't ooze out the side while cooking.

5 Angle the chicken breasts in a baking dish so they are partially upright and leaning against each other. Bake for 35 to 40 minutes, until the skin is browned and crispy and the chicken is cooked through.

SUBSTITUTIONS

Chicken Breasts	1 (2-pound/910 g) pork loin roast	A boneless half turkey breast (2 to 3 pounds/910 g to 1.4 kg), cut into 4 pieces
Goat Cheese	¼ cup/35 g crumbled Gorgonzola cheese	¼ cup/40 g crumbled feta cheese
Cranberries	¼ cup/35 g dried cherries, chopped	¼ cup/30 g dried blueberries

SHEET-PAN HARVEST CHICKEN

This sheet-pan dinner has all the flavors of fall, but with ingredients that are readily available year-round, so you can conjure a taste of Thanksgiving any time of the year. The beauty of cooking everything together on a sheet pan, aside from the ease of cleanup, is that you end up with a dish that is more than the sum of its parts; the flavors blend and meld as the ingredients cook down and caramelize. The Brussels sprouts and sweet potatoes love the high heat required for this dish, but I prevent the rosemary from burning and drying out by chopping it finely. *Serves 4*

4 bone-in, skin-on chicken thighs

2 pounds/910 g sweet potatoes, peeled and cut into 1-inch/2.5 cm chunks

1 pound/455 g Brussels sprouts, trimmed and halved

3 cloves garlic, minced

2 tablespoons finely chopped fresh rosemary

¼ cup/60 ml olive oil

1 teaspoon kosher salt

½ teaspoon coarsely ground black pepper

1 Preheat the oven to 375°F/190°C.

2 Add the chicken, sweet potatoes, Brussels sprouts, garlic, and rosemary to a large bowl. Drizzle the olive oil over, sprinkle with the salt and pepper, and stir well to combine.

3 Turn out the contents of the bowl onto a sheet pan, making sure the chicken is skin side up and the vegetables are evenly scattered around the chicken thighs.

4 Roast for 40 to 45 minutes, until the chicken and vegetables are nicely browned and the juices from the chicken run clear when a thigh is pricked with a knife.

SUBSTITUTIONS

Chicken Thighs	4 (¾-inch/2 cm thick) bone-in pork loin chops	2 pounds/910 g flank steak
Sweet Potatoes	2 pounds/910 g Yukon Gold potatoes	2 pounds/910 g parsnips, peeled
Rosemary	2 teaspoons minced fresh sage	1 tablespoon chopped fresh thyme

BACON-WRAPPED BUFFALO CHICKEN

Have you ever wished you could have Buffalo chicken wings as a main course, without feeling as if your mouth might literally go up in flames? This is the more palatable, main-course–friendly version using chicken breasts, which get a quick brushing of hot sauce and are then stuffed with a combination of blue and cream cheese and wrapped with bacon. The crispy, creamy spiciness of the chicken makes any sauce or side seem beside the point. *Serves 4*

4 boneless, skinless chicken breasts

¼ cup/60 ml hot sauce, such as Frank's

½ teaspoon kosher salt

¼ teaspoon freshly ground black pepper

4 ounces/115 g cream cheese, softened

¼ cup/35 g crumbled blue cheese

8 slices bacon

1 Preheat the oven to 375°F/190°C.

2 Cut a slit down the length of the thicker side of each chicken breast as deep as you can without cutting the breast in half. Place the chicken in a large bowl and season with the hot sauce, salt, and pepper, rubbing them in well so the meat absorbs the liquid.

3 In a small bowl, mash together the cream cheese and blue cheese.

4 Stuff one quarter of the cheese mixture into each chicken breast. Wrap each chicken breast with 2 slices of the bacon, tucking the ends underneath the chicken.

5 Place the chicken on a sheet pan and bake for 30 to 35 minutes, until the bacon is crispy and the juices run clear when the chicken is pricked with a knife.

SUBSTITUTIONS

Hot Sauce	½ cup/120 ml barbecue sauce	½ cup/120 ml honey-mustard dressing
Blue Cheese	¼ cup/40 g crumbled feta cheese	¼ cup/30 g shredded cheddar cheese

GREEK LEMON CHICKEN

I always pick up a pack of chicken thighs when I'm at the market. The result is that I'm often looking for new ways to prepare said thighs. This dish is crispy, fresh, and boldly flavored. It's healthy too, since the lemon adds a lot of flavor without any calories.

Garlic and cilantro would be great additions, and it's fine to swap in lime for the lemon if that's what you have on hand. It just doesn't get any simpler or more satisfying than this. *Serves 6*

---

6 bone-in, skin-on chicken thighs

¼ teaspoon kosher salt

¼ teaspoon coarsely ground black pepper

2 tablespoons lemon juice

3 cloves garlic, minced

⅓ cup/80 ml olive tapenade

2 ounces/55 g feta cheese, cut into ½-inch/13 mm cubes (about ¼ cup)

1 Preheat the oven to 375°F/190°C.

2 Pat the chicken thighs dry with a paper towel, then season with the salt and pepper, lemon juice, and garlic and place in a medium baking dish. Spoon the olive tapenade around the chicken and place the chunks of feta on top of the tapenade (be careful not to place the cheese on top of the chicken, as this would prevent even browning).

3 Bake for 30 to 35 minutes, until the chicken is browned and the feta is golden.

SUBSTITUTIONS

Chicken Thighs	6 bone-in pork loin chops
Olive Tapenade	1 cup/155 g pitted Kalamata olives
Feta Cheese	6 ounces/170 g (1½ cups) halloumi, cubed

SHEET-PAN FLANK STEAK

This easy sheet-pan meal is as quick to cook as it is delicious. My secret to making sure each ingredient is cooked perfectly is to parcook the Brussels sprouts first in the microwave. Flank steak is a flavorful but lean cut, and the Parmesan, along with a little olive oil, adds a little extra fat to protect it from the high heat. *Serves 6*

1 (2-pound/910 g) flank steak

2 tablespoons olive oil

2 teaspoons kosher salt

1 teaspoon coarsely ground black pepper

2 cloves garlic, minced

FOR THE BRUSSELS SPROUTS

2 pounds/910 g Brussels sprouts, trimmed and halved

½ teaspoon kosher salt

¼ teaspoon coarsely ground black pepper

½ cup/50 g grated Parmesan cheese

1 cup/90 g panko (Japanese bread crumbs)

4 tablespoons/55 g unsalted butter, melted

1 Preheat the oven to 450°F/230°C.

2 Rub the steak with the olive oil, then season it on both sides with the salt, pepper, and garlic. Place the steak in the middle of a sheet pan and set aside.

3 Add the Brussels sprouts to a microwave-safe bowl and cover with a wet paper towel. Microwave on high for 5 to 6 minutes, until the sprouts are softened and easily pierced with a knife.

4 In a large bowl, combine the salt, pepper, Parmesan, and panko, then add the parcooked Brussels sprouts and toss to combine. Add the melted butter and stir gently.

5 Distribute the Brussels sprouts around the steak and place in the oven. Cook for 5 minutes, then flip the steak and cook for about 5 minutes longer. The internal temperature of the steak should register 135°F/57°C for medium-rare or 140°F/60°C for medium when tested with a meat thermometer. (The steak will continue to cook once it's removed.)

6 Let the steak rest for 10 minutes, loosely tented with foil, before thinly slicing it against the grain and serving.

SUBSTITUTIONS

Flank Steak	2 boneless rib-eye steaks (2 pounds/910 g)	4 to 6 salmon fillets (about 2 pounds/910 g)
Brussels Sprouts	2 medium zucchini, halved lengthwise and sliced into ½-inch/13 mm thick slices	4 Roma (plum) tomatoes, quartered
Panko	¼ cup/60 ml balsamic vinegar (add in Step 4)	1 cup/90 g Ritz cracker crumbs

PORK CHOPS WITH PARMESAN AND ROOT VEGETABLES

Pork chops take beautifully to roasting. They cook evenly, and in this dish, they render just enough fat to flavor their oven mates: potatoes, garlic, and parsnips. Parsnips, if you're not used to cooking with them, lend a subtle sweetness and caramelize and crisp up when roasted. They are a great counterpoint to the earthiness of the potatoes and the savory pork. You can add any number of herbs here along with or instead of the garlic; oregano and thyme would both work well. *Serves 4*

4 bone-in pork loin chops, about 1 inch/2.5 cm thick (about 2 pounds/ 910 g total)

4 cloves garlic, minced

2 pounds/910 g Yukon Gold potatoes, scrubbed and cut into 1-inch/2.5 cm chunks

2 pounds/910 g parsnips, peeled and cut into 1-inch/2.5 cm chunks

1 teaspoon kosher salt

½ teaspoon coarsely ground black pepper

¼ cup/60 ml olive oil

⅓ cup/30 g grated Parmesan cheese

1 Preheat the oven to 375°F/190°C.

2 Add the pork chops, garlic, and cut-up vegetables to a large bowl. Season with the salt and pepper, drizzle the olive oil over, and mix well to ensure that the vegetables and pork are evenly coated with oil.

3 Transfer the chops to a sheet pan. Add the Parmesan to the vegetables and mix well, then scatter the vegetables around the chops.

4 Transfer to the oven and roast for 30 to 35 minutes, until the vegetables are cooked through and golden brown, and the thickest part of the pork registers 145°F/65°C on a meat thermometer.

SUBSTITUTIONS

Pork Chops	4 bone-in, skin-on chicken thighs	2 pounds/910 g (13–15 count) shrimp, peeled and deveined (cook for 20 minutes)
Yukon Gold Potatoes	2 pounds/910 g russet potatoes	2 cups/160 g panko (Japanese bread crumbs), to coat the shrimp
Parsnips	1 pound/455 g green beans, trimmed	1 pint/290 g grape tomatoes

BAKED BROWN RICE WITH VEGETABLES

If you think of brown rice as bland, too dense, or hard to cook, let this recipe change your mind. The secret is baking the rice and replacing the usual water with chicken broth, which adds a ton of flavor and results in fluffy, perfectly cooked rice. If you have Better Than Bouillon on hand, that works really well here. If you want to keep it vegetarian, substitute vegetable broth. I've made this with any number of vegetables, and pearl onions are delicious if you can find them, but feel free to adapt this to incorporate your favorites. *Serves 4*

1½ cups/270 g brown rice

½ teaspoon kosher salt

¼ teaspoon coarsely ground black pepper

5 carrots, peeled and cut into 1-inch/2.5 cm chunks

1 yellow onion, chopped

1 pound/455 g green beans, trimmed

2 tablespoons unsalted butter (optional)

3 cups/710 ml chicken broth, boiling hot

1 Preheat the oven to 375°F/190°C.

2 Add the rice to a Dutch oven, then add the salt and pepper. Scatter the carrots, onion, and green beans over the rice. If you're using the butter, cut it into small pieces and distribute them evenly over the vegetables.

3 Carefully pour the boiling-hot broth over the rice. Cover the pot, transfer to the oven, and bake for 60 minutes.

4 Remove the pot from the oven and let it sit for 5 minutes, then uncover, fluff the rice, and serve.

SMOKY CREAMED CORN

This is a bit of a choose-your-own-adventure side dish when it comes to the spiciness. Cooking the jalapeños with the corn in the bacon fat and butter will dim the heat and bring out the natural smokiness of the peppers—a nice complement for the bacon. Leaving the peppers raw and adding them at the end will make for a hotter, more spicy dish. And, of course, you can omit the jalapeños entirely and substitute a small green or red bell pepper, which would be lovely.

This is a rich and satisfying side; just a small portion goes a long way. It's best served alongside a lean main, like grilled chicken or shrimp. *Serves 4*

4 slices bacon, chopped

2 tablespoons unsalted butter

1 jalapeño, seeded and chopped

1 (16-ounce/455 g) bag frozen sweet yellow corn kernels or kernels cut from 3 ears of corn

1½ cups/355 ml half-and-half (or ¾ cup/180 ml whole milk plus ¾ cup/ 180 ml heavy cream)

1 tablespoon all-purpose flour

½ teaspoon salt

¼ teaspoon coarsely ground black pepper

1 tablespoon sugar (optional)

1 Put the bacon in a large skillet set over medium heat and cook until just beginning to crisp but still chewy. Remove from the pan with a slotted spoon and set aside.

2 Remove all but 1 tablespoon of bacon fat from the pan, melt the butter, then add the jalapeño and corn and cook for 3 to 4 minutes, stirring occasionally.

3 Meanwhile, in a large bowl, whisk together the half-and-half, flour, salt, and pepper.

4 Pour the half-and-half mixture into the pan, whisking constantly, and cook for 6 to 8 minutes, stirring occasionally, until the mixture thickens. Taste and adjust the seasonings as needed. If you find your corn isn't very sweet, you can add 1 tablespoon sugar. Sprinkle the bacon over the creamed corn just before serving.

SESAME-SOY GREEN BEANS

Sautéed green beans are a reliable side dish, but when you're looking to mix things up a bit, you might try turning to two ingredients you likely already have in your pantry: soy sauce and sesame oil. I particularly like this combination when I want a side to accompany an Asian-inspired dish, but the flavors are so pleasing, they transcend categories. If you want a less assertively flavored dish, you can replace half the sesame oil with vegetable oil. *Serves 4*

1 tablespoon
vegetable oil

2 teaspoons sesame
oil

1 pound/455 g green
beans, trimmed

2 cloves garlic, minced

2 tablespoons soy
sauce

2 teaspoons white
sesame seeds

1 Place a large skillet over medium heat, add the vegetable and sesame oils, and allow them to heat for a minute or two. Add the green beans and cook, stirring occasionally, for 5 minutes, or until they are tender-crisp. Add the garlic, stir, and cook until fragrant, 2 to 3 minutes.

2 Add the soy sauce and toss, then cook for 1 minute more. Garnish with the sesame seeds.

MACARONI AND CHEESE

This is my perfect blank-canvas mac and cheese. It's delicious as is, or make it your own with any number of add-ins—minced jalapeños, Cajun seasoning, or diced rotisserie chicken; it's highly versatile.

I use cheddar cheese here, but many people like mac and cheese made with American cheese. The processed cheese will always be creamier, but this version is no less delicious. If you want some of that nostalgic taste, you can use half Velveeta and half cheddar. It's best not to use pre-shredded cheese, which often has cellulose added to it and will make for a grainy mac and cheese. Start with a block of cheese instead. *Serves 8*

1 teaspoon kosher salt, plus more for the pasta cooking water

1 pound/455 g elbow macaroni

4 tablespoons/55 g unsalted butter

¼ cup/30 g all-purpose flour

½ teaspoon ground mustard

¼ teaspoon coarsely ground black pepper

2 cups/475 ml whole milk

8 ounces/225 g cheddar cheese, shredded (2 cups)

1 Bring a large pot of heavily salted water to a boil. Add the pasta and cook according to the package directions; drain and set aside.

2 Add the butter to the empty pasta pot and melt it over medium heat. Whisk in the flour, 1 teaspoon salt, mustard, and pepper and cook, whisking, for 1 minute, or until the flour begins to bubble.

3 Very slowly pour in the milk, whisking continuously. Bring the mixture to a low simmer and cook for 6 to 8 minutes, until it has thickened slightly. Add the cheese and whisk well until melted and thoroughly combined.

4 Add the pasta to the sauce and give it a good stir. Cook for 1 minute to bring the pasta back up to temperature, then serve immediately.

HONEY-GINGER CARROTS

This is a riff on Ina Garten's Indonesian Honey-Garlic Chicken. As a side dish, it works with so many different vegetables; in place of the carrots, try zucchini, asparagus, broccoli, bok choy, or eggplant (though you may want to sear the sliced eggplant first to prevent it from absorbing all the honey). Or turn this into a vegetarian main dish with tofu and serve over rice, or a meaty main with chicken or pork. Any leftover sauce holds up really well—so well that it can be frozen and then defrosted when needed. For even more of a flavor punch, use lemongrass in place of the ginger, or agave or brown sugar instead of the honey. *Serves 4*

6 carrots, peeled and cut into ½-inch/ 13 mm slices

¼ cup/60 ml honey

3 tablespoons soy sauce

3 cloves garlic, minced

1 tablespoon minced fresh ginger

1 Add the carrots and 1 cup/235 ml water to a large skillet with a tight-fitting lid, cover, and steam over high heat for 5 minutes.

2 Remove the lid and let all the water cook off, 3 to 4 minutes.

3 Add the honey, soy sauce, garlic, and ginger and stir well. Cook for 4 to 5 minutes, until the sauce has thickened and the carrots are well glazed.

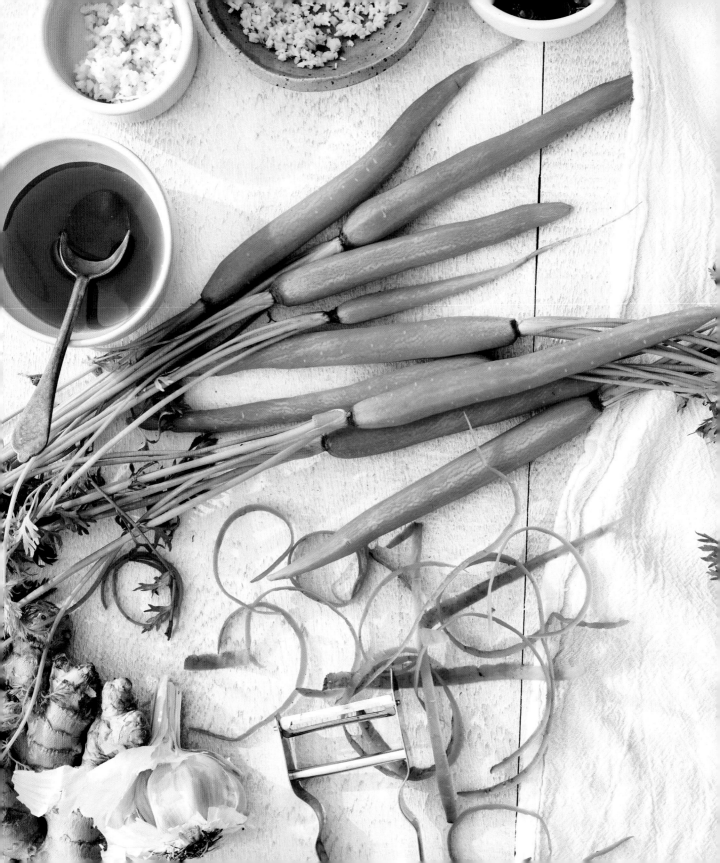

CHEESY CREAMY SPINACH

This decadent dish is one of my favorite holiday sides, and its garlicky punch stands up well to a roast or other meaty main course. I love how rich and creamy it is, but if you'd like to lighten it up, use half-and-half in place of the heavy cream (don't use milk, or you'll end up with a runny dish). Feel free to substitute provolone or mozzarella for the Gruyère. *Serves 6*

4 tablespoons/55 g unsalted butter

1 large yellow onion, chopped

1 cup/235 ml heavy cream

30 ounces/850 g frozen spinach, thawed, drained, chopped, and squeezed dry

½ teaspoon kosher salt

¼ teaspoon coarsely ground black pepper

1 cup/100 g grated Parmesan cheese

½ cup/55 g grated Gruyère cheese

1 Melt the butter in a large Dutch oven over medium heat. Add the onion and cook until translucent, 10 to 12 minutes.

2 Whisk in the heavy cream, bring to a simmer, and cook for 5 to 7 minutes.

3 Add the spinach to the pot and stir well to combine. Add the salt, pepper, Parmesan, and Gruyère cheese and whisk well. Cook until the sauce is thick and creamy, 2 to 3 minutes.

CHEDDAR BROCCOLI BAKE

I love ordering vegetable fritto misto when I'm at an Italian restaurant. This dish has the same appeal as that breaded and fried appetizer, but it's baked. In order to achieve the delicate crunch, I toss the broccoli with vegetable oil so the florets will really grab the cheese for even coating. Pulse the cheddar and Parmesan cheese along with the bread crumbs in a food processor so the pieces are just the right size. To ensure the coated broccoli browns nicely, you can give them a quick spray with vegetable oil right before they go in the oven. *Serves 4*

¾ cup/85 g shredded cheddar cheese

1 cup/100 g bread crumbs

½ cup/50 g grated Parmesan cheese

1 (1-ounce/28 g) packet ranch seasoning

4 cups/365 g broccoli florets

3 tablespoons vegetable oil

1 Preheat the oven to 400°F/205°C.

2 Add the cheddar cheese to a food processor fitted with the metal blade and pulse until it is the size of small crumbs. Add the bread crumbs, Parmesan, and ranch seasoning and pulse until the mixture is evenly combined and looks like a dry crumble.

3 In a large bowl, toss the broccoli with the oil, then add the bread crumb mixture and stir well.

4 Turn the broccoli out onto a sheet pan, spreading it out in a single layer. Roast for 30 to 35 minutes, until browned and crispy.

FRENCH FRIES WITH BLUE CHEESE GRAVY

French fries with a rich, cheesy sauce is one of the most decadent, most satisfying dishes on earth. Tangy and creamy, crispy and starchy—every one of your taste buds will be firing. That one meal before I die—this is it.

When it comes to the french fries, you can go a couple ways. Open a bag of frozen fries and pop them in a hot oven, no judgment here. Or, you can make the fries yourself. If you go this route, the recipe provides tips on how to achieve the best version of an oven fry.

I serve these alongside steak for a classic combination. But this gravy is so incredible it can be used in a million ways: Try it as a dipping sauce for potato chips, or serve it over mashed potatoes, pork chops, or roasted mushrooms. You cannot go wrong. *Serves 4*

FOR THE FRIES

2 pounds/910 g russet potatoes, peeled and cut into ½-inch/ 13 mm thick sticks

3 tablespoons vegetable oil

½ teaspoon kosher salt

¼ teaspoon coarsely ground black pepper

1 Preheat the oven to 400°F/205°C.

2 Soak the potatoes in cold water for 20 to 30 minutes to leach out the extra starch. Drain and dry them carefully.

3 In a large bowl, toss the potatoes with the oil, salt, and pepper. Arrange in a single layer on a sheet pan. Don't crowd the pan, or you'll end up steaming, not roasting, the potatoes.

4 Roast the potatoes for 25 minutes, then toss and roast for another 10 to 15 minutes, or until browned and crispy.

FOR THE BLUE CHEESE GRAVY

4 tablespoons/55 g unsalted butter

½ yellow onion, minced

½ teaspoon kosher salt

¼ teaspoon coarsely ground black pepper

1 cup/235 ml heavy cream

2 tablespoons Worcestershire sauce

1 cup/135 g crumbled blue cheese

5 While the potatoes are cooking, make the blue cheese gravy: Melt the butter in a large skillet over medium-high heat. Add the onion, salt, and pepper and cook until the onion is translucent, 6 to 8 minutes.

6 Add the heavy cream and Worcestershire sauce and bring to a simmer, then cook for 5 to 6 minutes.

7 Add the blue cheese and whisk well until the cheese is melted and fully incorporated. Remove from the heat.

8 Transfer the fries to a shallow serving dish and pour the gravy over the top, or transfer the gravy to a small bowl and serve alongside.

CHAPTER THREE

7 *Ingredient*

DINNERS

MUSHROOM STROGANOFF

With apologies to my vegetarian friends, meat is the key to the success of so many of my recipes. I just love it, and it's where my heart is. But that is why this vegetarian recipe was such a win for me—and to be honest, such a surprise. The cremini mushrooms bring such depth and intensity to the dish, and marry so perfectly with the creamy sauce, I wouldn't dream of adding meat.

Stroganoff is my definition of family food. It's endlessly comforting—and this version can be made in under 30 minutes. *Serves 4*

½ teaspoon kosher salt, plus more for the pasta cooking water

1 pound/455 g wide egg noodles

8 tablespoons (1 stick)/115 g unsalted butter

1 pound/455 g cremini mushrooms, sliced

¼ teaspoon coarsely ground black pepper

1 large shallot, minced

3 tablespoons all-purpose flour

1½ cups/355 ml vegetable broth, or as needed

1 cup/235 ml white wine

½ cup/120 ml sour cream

parsley for garnish

1 Bring a large pot of heavily salted water to a boil. Add the noodles and cook for 1 minute shy of the package directions. Drain and set aside.

2 Melt the butter in a large skillet over medium-high heat. Add the mushrooms, salt, and pepper and cook for 2 to 3 minutes without stirring, allowing the mushrooms to brown slightly. Stir, then cook for another 2 to 3 minutes without stirring to brown them well. Stir the mushrooms, add the shallot, and cook for another minute.

3 Add the flour and stir well to combine, then add the vegetable broth and white wine, bring to a simmer, and cook for 6 to 8 minutes, until reduced by about half. Add the sour cream, stirring until fully combined, then add the noodles and stir to coat with the sauce. If the sauce seems too thick, thin with a little additional vegetable stock.

SUBSTITUTIONS

Egg Noodles	4 cups/820 g cooked white rice	no change to recipe
Shallot	1 red onion, diced	1 yellow onion, diced
Flour	2 tablespoons cornstarch, dissolved in 1 tablespoon cool water	no change to recipe
Vegetable Broth	1½ cups/355 ml beef broth	no change to recipe
Sour Cream	4 ounces/115 g cream cheese plus ¼ cup/60 ml water	no change to recipe

7-INGREDIENT DINNERS 133

CREAMY CAJUN PASTA

I'll admit it, this is heavily inspired by the Cheesecake Factory's Cajun Jambalaya Pasta. My version replaces the tomato (red) sauce with a white sauce made from wine, heavy cream, and Parmesan cheese. I reach for any opportunity to use Cajun seasoning, a mainstay of my pantry. I promise, this lively little dish will appeal to everyone at your table. *Serves 4*

½ teaspoon kosher salt, plus more for the pasta cooking water

8 ounces/225 g penne

2 tablespoons vegetable oil, plus more for the pasta

2 boneless, skinless chicken breasts

¼ teaspoon coarsely ground black pepper

3 cloves garlic, minced

2 tablespoons Cajun seasoning, plus more for sprinkling

½ cup/120 ml white wine

½ cup/120 ml heavy cream

¾ cup/75 g grated Parmesan cheese, plus more for serving

1 Bring a large pot of heavily salted water to a boil. Add the pasta and cook for 1 minute shy of the package directions. Drain, reserving ½ cup/120 ml of the pasta water. Put the cooked pasta in a bowl and toss with some oil to prevent sticking.

2 Cut the chicken into thin strips and season with the salt and pepper.

3 Heat the 2 tablespoons oil in a large skillet over medium-high heat. When it is hot, add the chicken and cook until browned, 3 to 4 minutes per side.

4 Add the garlic and Cajun seasoning, stir well, and cook for 30 seconds, or until fragrant.

5 Add the reserved pasta water and the white wine, bring to a simmer, and simmer for 8 to 10 minutes, until the liquid has reduced by half.

6 Add the heavy cream and Parmesan cheese, stir well, and cook for 3 to 4 minutes, until the sauce has further reduced and thickened.

7 Add the pasta and stir to coat. Serve with an extra sprinkling of Parmesan cheese and Cajun seasoning, if desired.

SUBSTITUTIONS

Penne	8 ounces/225 g thin spaghetti	no change to recipe
Chicken	4 links pork sausage, sliced into rounds	2 bell peppers, thinly sliced

GARLIC SHRIMP WITH OYSTER SAUCE

This is a re-creation of one of my favorite special-occasion dishes from childhood. It relies on two pantry staples—oyster sauce and sesame oil—which give it a strong punch of flavor. Along with water chestnuts, bell peppers, and juicy shrimp, it hits all the notes of crunchy, salty, and sweet. Perfect for any night, special occasion or not! *Serves 6*

3 tablespoons vegetable oil

2 teaspoons sesame oil

2 pounds/910 g shrimp (13–15 count) peeled, tail section removed, and deveined

¼ teaspoon kosher salt

1 red bell pepper, cored, seeded, and thinly sliced

1 cup/90 g broccoli florets

1 (8-ounce/225 g) can sliced water chestnuts, drained

2 cloves garlic, minced

⅓ cup/80 ml oyster sauce

1 Add the vegetable oil and sesame oil to a large skillet set over high heat. Once the oil is hot, add the shrimp and cook for 1 minute on each side, or until bright pink. Using a slotted spoon, remove the shrimp from the skillet.

2 Lower the heat to medium-high, add the salt, bell pepper, broccoli, and water chestnuts, and cook for 3 to 4 minutes, until the pepper has softened slightly.

3 Add the garlic and cook for 30 seconds, or until fragrant. Add the oyster sauce and 1 tablespoon water, stir well, and cook for another minute or two.

4 Return the shrimp to the skillet and stir until the shrimp is well coated and warmed through.

SUBSTITUTIONS

Sesame Oil	no change to recipe	¼ cup/60 ml low-sodium soy sauce, added in Step 4
Shrimp	3 boneless, skinless chicken breasts, thinly sliced	1 (2-pound/910 g) boneless pork loin roast, thinly sliced
Broccoli	1 cup/70 g sliced bok choy	1 cup/63 g snow peas
Water Chestnuts	1 (8-ounce/225 g) can bamboo shoots, drained	8 ounces/225 g mushrooms, sliced
Garlic	1 tablespoon garlic-ginger paste	no change to recipe
Oyster Sauce	no change to recipe	⅓ cup/80 ml peanut butter

CARIBBEAN CHILE SHRIMP

I love Caribbean flavors, especially jerk seasoning. If you have a favorite premade jerk seasoning, you're welcome to use that, but I like making my own pared-down version, with just four ingredients. Here the sweetness and slight tanginess of the mango is a great foil for the kick of the cayenne, as is the subtle sweetness of the bell pepper. I'm someone who always has frozen mango in my freezer for my morning smoothie, but fresh works just as well. If you do go with frozen, I suggest defrosting it in the microwave and then draining off the liquid, so it doesn't dilute the flavor of the final dish. *Serves 4*

1 pound/455 g (13–15 count) shrimp, peeled and deveined

¼ teaspoon kosher salt

⅛ teaspoon coarsely ground black pepper

¼ teaspoon cayenne

¼ teaspoon ground turmeric

2 tablespoons vegetable oil

1 mango, peeled, pitted, and cut into ½-inch/13 mm chunks, or 1 cup/93 g frozen mango, thawed and drained

1 red bell pepper, cored, seeded, and cut into ½-inch/ 13 mm pieces

2 green onions, thinly sliced

1 teaspoon chopped fresh thyme or ¼ teaspoon dried thyme

1 In a medium bowl, toss the shrimp with the salt, pepper, cayenne, and turmeric. Refrigerate, covered, for 20 minutes.

2 Heat the oil in a large skillet over medium-high heat. Once the oil is hot, add the shrimp and cook for 1 minute, then flip and cook for another minute. Transfer the shrimp to a clean bowl.

3 Add the mango, bell pepper, and green onions to the skillet and cook for 2 to 3 minutes, until the bell pepper and green onions start to soften.

4 Return the shrimp to the pan along with the thyme, toss to combine, and cook for 1 minute more, or until the shrimp is heated through.

SUBSTITUTIONS

Shrimp	4 boneless, skinless chicken breasts	4 (6-ounce/170 g) bone-in pork loin chops
Cayenne	¼ teaspoon chili powder	no change to recipe
Mango	1 cup/165 g chopped pineapple	no change to recipe

DIJON SALMON

The combination of wine, balsamic vinegar, and Dijon creates a very sophisticated sauce. The mustard loses some of its intensity when it cooks and falls to the background, making for a more nuanced flavor. It would be just as delicious as a salad dressing or served alongside grilled chicken breasts. *Serves 4*

3 cloves garlic

⅓ cup/80 ml balsamic vinegar

2 tablespoons white wine

2 tablespoons honey

1 tablespoon Dijon mustard

1 tablespoon fresh lemon juice

4 (6-ounce/170 g) salmon fillets, skin-on

½ teaspoon kosher salt

¼ teaspoon coarsely ground black pepper

1 tablespoon olive oil

1 Add the garlic, balsamic vinegar, white wine, honey, Dijon, and lemon juice to a food processor and pulse until smooth, about 30 seconds.

2 Season the salmon with the salt and pepper. Heat the olive oil in a large skillet over medium-high heat. Once the oil is hot, add the salmon skin side down and cook for 4 minutes. Flip the salmon and cook for another minute.

3 Pour the mustard sauce over the salmon and cook for 2 minutes more.

4 Remove the salmon from the pan and cook the sauce for 3 to 4 minutes more, until thickened. Serve the salmon with the sauce spooned over the top.

SUBSTITUTIONS

Balsamic Vinegar	¼ cup/60 ml white wine vinegar	no change to recipe
Honey	3 tablespoons maple syrup	no change to recipe
Dijon Mustard	1 tablespoon hot and sweet mustard	no change to recipe
Salmon	2 pounds/910 g (13–15 count) shrimp, peeled and deveined	4 boneless, skinless chicken breasts, butterflied (see page 96 for instructions)

TIP: *To prevent fish from sticking to the pan when you pan-sear it, make sure your pan is well coated with oil or butter, and make sure the fat is hot. I look for ripples in the oil as an indicator; you can also drop a small piece of fish in to see if it sizzles. Then, once you add the fish, it's important to just leave it to sear and not try to move it. The timing will vary, but typically it takes about 4 minutes to get a nice sear. Once you've seared the first side, check to make sure there's still enough oil/butter in the pan; if not, add a touch more before flipping the fish. Make sure the oil/butter has a few seconds to come up to temperature before you flip the fish.*

THAI CHICKEN SKILLET

This is bright and light thanks to a double dose of lime—zest and juice—and Thai green curry paste, which has a refreshing tang. And unlike curries that use coconut milk as their base, this one isn't heavy. I make it with just about any ground meat—chicken, beef, or pork. If you'd like to try making this with shrimp, I suggest mincing it to simulate the texture of ground meat. Serve over rice with shredded cabbage, or even as the filling for a burrito. *Serves 4*

2 tablespoons
vegetable oil

1 pound/455 g
ground chicken
(not extra-lean)

½ teaspoon kosher
salt

¼ teaspoon coarsely
ground black pepper

2 cloves garlic, minced

1 cup/63 g snow peas

2 carrots, peeled and
cut into ¼-inch/6 mm
coins

2 tablespoons Thai
green curry paste

Grated zest and
juice of 1 lime (about
2 tablespoons juice)

1 cup/235 ml chicken
broth (or 1 tablespoon
Better Than Bouillon
chicken base mixed
with 1 cup/235 ml
water)

1 Heat the vegetable oil in a large skillet over medium-high heat. Once the oil is hot, add the ground chicken, salt, and pepper and cook, breaking apart the chicken with a spoon, until browned, 4 to 5 minutes.

2 Add the garlic, snow peas, and carrots and cook for 3 to 4 minutes, until the vegetables are softened.

3 Add the green curry paste, lime zest and juice, and chicken broth, bring to a simmer, and let simmer for 4 to 5 minutes, until the liquid has cooked down and the vegetables are tender.

SUBSTITUTIONS

Ground Chicken	1 pound/455 g ground pork	1 pound/455 g (13–15 count) shrimp, peeled, deveined, and minced	4 (6-ounce/170 g) skinless salmon fillets
Garlic	1 tablespoon minced fresh lemongrass	no change to recipe	no change to recipe
Snow Peas	1 cup/90 g broccoli florets	1 cup/70 g sliced bok choy	no change to recipe
Lime (zest and juice)	¼ cup/10 g chopped fresh basil	no change to recipe	no change to recipe
Chicken Broth	no change to recipe	1 (13.5-ounce/ 400 ml) can coconut milk	1 (13.5-ounce/ 400 ml) can coconut milk

SAUTÉED PORK WITH PEANUT SAUCE IN LETTUCE CUPS

Sure, you could serve this delectable dish over rice, but serving it in lettuce cups makes it a lighter meal. If you're looking to lighten this up in another way, you could replace half the pork with water chestnuts, bamboo shoots, mushrooms, or zucchini. *Serves 4*

1 tablespoon vegetable oil

1 pound/455 g ground pork

2 cloves garlic, minced

1 tablespoon minced fresh ginger

2 teaspoons sesame oil

¼ cup/60 ml low-sodium soy sauce

¼ cup/60 ml peanut butter

1 head butter lettuce for serving, reserve extra for leftovers

Shredded carrots and/or sliced green onions and radishes for serving (optional)

FOR THE SAUCE (OPTIONAL)

2 tablespoons rice vinegar

1 tablespoon vegetable oil

½ teaspoon sesame oil

1 tablespoon minced or sliced bird's-eye chile

1 Heat the vegetable oil in a large skillet over medium-high heat. When the oil is hot, add the pork and cook, breaking it apart, until it is well browned, 4 to 5 minutes.

2 Add the garlic, ginger, and sesame oil, stir well, and cook for 1 minute, or until fragrant.

3 Add the soy sauce and peanut butter and stir until the sauce has thickened and the pork is evenly coated.

4 To serve, scoop a few spoonfuls of the pork into each lettuce cup and enjoy as is, or top with shredded carrots and/or sliced green onions and radishes. If making the sauce, mix the ingredients in a small bowl and serve alongside.

SUBSTITUTIONS

Ground Pork	1 pound/455 g ground chicken (not extra-lean)	1 pound/455 g ground turkey (not extra-lean)
Sesame Oil	1 (8-ounce/225 g) can water chestnuts, drained and chopped	8 ounces/225 g mushrooms, diced
Peanut Butter	⅓ cup/80 ml hoisin sauce	¼ cup/60 ml oyster sauce
Lettuce	4 cups/820 g cooked white rice	8 ounces/225 g egg noodles, cooked

PEANUT BEEF SATAY

Peanut sauce is one of the tastiest and easiest Asian sauces and I use it as often as I can, on all types of meat, seafood, and chicken. In fact, I quadruple this recipe every time I make it, just so I'm sure to have some on hand for later use. It'll keep for a few weeks in the fridge. *Serves 6*

2 pounds/910 g boneless rib-eye steaks, thinly sliced (see Tip)

3 tablespoons vegetable oil

½ teaspoon kosher salt

¼ teaspoon coarsely ground black pepper

½ cup/120 ml smooth peanut butter

2 tablespoons low-sodium soy sauce

1 tablespoon honey

2 cloves garlic, minced

1 teaspoon minced fresh ginger

¼ cup/40 g unsalted roasted peanuts, chopped

TIP: *The trick to getting paper-thin, even slices is to put the beef in the freezer for 30 minutes before slicing it.*

1 Rub the beef with the vegetable oil, salt, and pepper.

2 Set a large skillet over medium-high heat. Once the pan is hot, add the beef and sear for 2 minutes on each side; work in batches, if necessary, to avoid overcrowding the skillet. Remove the beef from the pan and lower the heat to medium.

3 Add the peanut butter, soy sauce, honey, garlic, and ginger to the pan, whisking all the while, until thoroughly mixed, then cook for another 30 seconds.

4 Return the beef to the pan and give it all a good stir. Garnish with the peanuts before serving.

SUBSTITUTIONS

Rib-eye Steak	6 boneless, skinless chicken thighs	2 pounds/910 g (13–15 count) shrimp, peeled and deveined
Honey	1 tablespoon sugar	no change to recipe
Ginger	½ teaspoon ground ginger	no change to recipe

CRISPY COD WITH TARRAGON

Tarragon and seafood are such a harmonious combination it's as if they were made for each other. Add wine, and it's a match made in heaven. The cracker crumbs add a little texture, but you could just as easily use panko or even finely chopped nuts. There are versions of this kind of dish—a white fish seared and served in a buttery sauce—on most restaurant menus. People are often intimidated by making it at home, but it's actually quite easy to pull off. *Serves 4*

4 (6-ounce/170 g) cod fillets, skin-on

1 tablespoon all-purpose flour

¼ teaspoon kosher salt

¼ teaspoon coarsely ground black pepper

8 tablespoons (1 stick)/115 g unsalted butter

10 buttery round crackers, such as Ritz, crushed

¼ teaspoon paprika

Grated zest and juice of 1 lemon (about 3 tablespoons juice)

¼ cup/60 ml white wine

¼ cup/13 g chopped fresh tarragon

1 Coat the cod lightly with the flour, then season with the salt and pepper.

2 Add 3 tablespoons of the butter to a large skillet set over medium-high heat. Once the butter has melted, add the cod skin side down and cook for 3 minutes. Flip and cook on the other side for another 3 minutes. Remove the fish from the pan and cover to keep warm.

3 Add 3 more tablespoons of the butter to the pan, and once it has melted, add the cracker crumbs and paprika and stir and toast for 30 seconds. Remove from the pan and set aside.

4 Add the remaining 2 tablespoons butter to the pan, along with the lemon zest, juice, and wine and cook until the liquid has reduced by half, 5 to 6 minutes. Stir in the tarragon.

5 Return the fish to the pan to rewarm it, spooning over the sauce. Top with the buttery cracker topping just before serving.

SUBSTITUTIONS

Cod	4 (6-ounce/170 g) sea bass fillets, skin on	4 boneless, skinless chicken breasts
Crackers	1 cup/80 g panko (Japanese bread crumbs)	no change to recipe
Tarragon	1 tablespoon chopped fresh thyme	no change to recipe

Classic Recipe
ULTIMATE POT ROAST

The most important thing to know before embarking on this recipe is how to select the right piece of meat. Look for a roast that is at least 2 to 3 inches/ 5 to 7 cm thick and with good, even marbling throughout. I avoid pieces that have big sections of fat with expanses of lean meat in between (see photos, page 16). Once you've chosen the right piece of meat, you're more than halfway there.

Next up is how to brown it. The more you allow your meat to brown, the better a crust it will develop, and the more tender and moist the roast will be. This step is so important, it pays to do it carefully. When I'm browning meat, I make sure to start with my meat at room temperature, not straight from the fridge. I let the oil heat until it's shimmering but not smoking, and then, once I've added the meat, I allow it to sear for 4 to 5 minutes on each side, without touching it.

Another key to the success of this dish is how well the meat is seasoned. I have a pretty heavy hand when it comes to salting meat, but don't be alarmed by the amount of salt I called for here. Some of that salt will end up in the liquid the meat cooks in, which will, in turn, season the carrots and potatoes that are cooking with the pot roast.

Cutting the potatoes and carrots the same size will ensure that they cook evenly and in the same amount of time. I love this with Yukon Gold potatoes. If you're adding any other vegetables, make sure they can hold up to the long cooking time. Other root vegetables like turnips, parsnips, or sweet potatoes work well. If you want more aromatics, add some onions cut into wedges or chunks of celery.

Once the beef is done, you can create a gravy from the cooking liquid. Remove the beef, spoon off any extra fat from the surface of the liquid, and then create a slurry of cornstarch and room temperature water to whisk into the meat juices.

The beef is ready when it is fork-tender. If you insert a fork and there's resistance, give it another hour or so. If you find that it's still not tender, then the cut of meat may be too lean. If that's the case, let the meat cool, cut it against the grain into thin strips, and serve it with the gravy. It will still be delicious.

NOTE: If you have a slow cooker with an aluminum insert, you can use that to brown the meat on the stovetop and then just re-insert it when you're ready to cook the roast. If your slow cooker doesn't have this feature, you can brown the meat in a skillet.

Serves 6 to 8

1 (4- to 5-pound/
1.8 to 2.3 kg)
chuck roast

2 teaspoons kosher
salt

1 teaspoon coarsely
ground black pepper

1 teaspoon dried
thyme

5 carrots, peeled and
cut into 2-inch/5 cm
chunks

2 pounds/910 g Yukon
Gold potatoes, peeled
and cut into 2-inch/
5 cm chunks

2 cloves garlic, minced

2 tablespoons
vegetable oil

2 cups/475 ml
beef broth

1 tablespoon
cornstarch

1 Season the chuck roast with the salt, pepper, and thyme.

2 Place the carrots, potatoes, and garlic in the bottom of the slow cooker. If you're using a slow cooker with insert (see Note, page 147), brown the meat before adding the vegetables.

3 Add the canola oil to a large heavy skillet and heat over medium-high heat. When the oil is very hot and shimmers, add the roast and brown deeply all over, 4 to 5 minutes on each side.

4 Once browned, transfer the roast to the slow cooker, setting it on top of the vegetables, and add the beef broth. Cook on low for 8 hours. The roast is done when the meat is fork-tender.

5 Remove the meat and use two forks to pull it apart into chunks.

6 To make gravy, once you've removed the meat, mix the cornstarch with 2 tablespoons water to make a slurry and add to the cooking liquid to thicken. Return the meat to the slow cooker and stir it into the gravy.

TIP: *If you don't have a slow cooker, you can make this in a Dutch oven. Cook, covered, for 3 hours at 325°F/165°C.*

SUBSTITUTIONS

Chuck Roast	1 5- to 6-pound/2.3 to 2/7 kg) boneless pork shoulder roast
Thyme	1 teaspoon dried oregano
Carrots	6 parsnips, cut into 2-inch/5 cm chunks
Yukon Gold Potatoes	1 yellow onion, sliced

STEWED MOROCCAN CHICKEN WITH SPINACH

This is an easy, flavorful, and filling stew. A few minutes of browning ensures the best flavor for the chicken, and adding the spinach just before serving gives the stew brightness and ensures a tender (not mushy) consistency. *Serves 4*

---

2 tablespoons vegetable oil

4 bone-in, skin-on chicken thighs

1 yellow onion, chopped

1 (15-ounce/425 g) can chickpeas, drained and rinsed

1 teaspoon kosher salt

¼ teaspoon coarsely ground black pepper

2 teaspoons ground cumin

1 teaspoon ground coriander

½ teaspoon ground cinnamon

1 (10-ounce/285 g) package frozen spinach, thawed, drained well, and squeezed dry

1 Preheat the oven to 325°F/165°C.

2 Heat a medium Dutch oven over medium-high heat, then add the oil. When the oil is hot, add the chicken skin side down and brown on both sides, about 4 minutes per side. Remove from the pot and set aside.

3 Add the onion to the Dutch oven and cook for 6 to 8 minutes, until the onion softens and begins to color. Then add the chickpeas.

4 Add the salt, pepper, cumin, coriander, and cinnamon and stir well. Nestle the chicken into the chickpeas and onion, skin side up, and add 2 cups/475 ml water.

5 Cover the pot, transfer to the oven, and bake for 1 hour.

6 Stir in the spinach, cover the pot, and cook for an additional 15 minutes.

SUBSTITUTIONS

Chicken Thighs	2 large eggplants, cut into 1-inch/ 2.5 cm cubes	2 pounds/910 g boneless pork shoulder, cut into 1-inch/2.5 cm chunks	2 pounds/910 g chuck roast, cut into 1-inch/2.5 cm chunks
Onion	1 red onion, diced	no change to recipe	no change to recipe
Chickpeas	1 (15-ounce/ 425 g) can cannellini beans, rinsed and drained	no change to recipe	no change to recipe
Spinach	5 carrots, peeled and diced	4 Yukon Gold potatoes, scrubbed and diced	no change to recipe

SLOW-COOKER SPAGHETTI AND MEATBALLS

Meatballs are just about universally loved, but the multistep, multipot process of making them can be a turnoff. The slow cooker eliminates the threat of a sink full of dirty dishes by transforming spaghetti and meatballs into a one-pot meal. I opt for a leaner beef for this recipe, so the meatballs don't end up bathed in a greasy sauce. If you're not using thin spaghetti, it may need longer than the 45 minutes to cook. *Serves 6*

2 pounds/910 g lean (85/15) ground beef

½ teaspoon kosher salt

¼ teaspoon coarsely ground black pepper

⅔ cup/65 g bread crumbs

½ cup/50 g grated Parmesan cheese, plus more for serving

3 cloves garlic, minced

1 teaspoon dried oregano

2 (24-ounce/680 g) jars marinara sauce

1 pound/455 g thin spaghetti

1 Add the ground beef, salt, pepper, bread crumbs, Parmesan cheese, garlic, and oregano to a bowl and mix well.

2 Measure out 3-tablespoon-sized portions of meat into your palm and roll into balls.

3 Pour half of a jar of marinara sauce into the slow cooker, then place the meatballs in the slow cooker and cover with the remaining sauce.

4 Cook on low for 7 hours.

5 Add the thin spaghetti to the slow cooker and cook for 45 minutes longer, or until the pasta is cooked through. Serve, sprinkled with additional Parmesan cheese.

SUBSTITUTIONS

Ground Beef	2 pounds/910 g ground chicken (not extra-lean)	2 pounds/910 g ground turkey (not extra-lean)
Bread Crumbs	1 cup/80 g panko (Japanese bread crumbs)	3 slices stale white bread, crumbled and soaked briefly in ¼ cup/60 ml milk
Oregano	1 teaspoon dried basil	no change to recipe

SLOW-COOKER BEEF CHILI

This chili is hearty and deeply satisfying. And, unlike many chili recipes, it doesn't call for a million ingredients. At its base are kidney beans, a personal favorite of mine—their thick skin holds up well to long cooking, and their beautiful red hue adds a nice pop of color. You can always swap in another bean, though—whatever you happen to have on hand. I make this in the slow cooker for its even cooking and the peace of mind it affords. However, slow cookers, as great as they are, do not excel at creating thick sauces. My solution is to add ground-up saltines, which thicken the sauce and add a little texture in the process. This simple and classic chili calls for a basic chili powder—and that's important, as anything else could add unwanted spice, smokiness, or competing flavors. I usually top this with sliced green onions and a dollop of sour cream, but any of the usual suspects would work: grated cheddar cheese, Fritos, or cornbread on the side. *Serves 6*

2 pounds/910 g lean ground beef

1 yellow onion, chopped

3 garlic cloves, minced

2 (15.5-ounce/440 g) cans red kidney beans, drained and rinsed

1 (28-ounce/795 g) can tomato sauce

3 tablespoons chili powder

1 teaspoon kosher salt

1 teaspoon coarsely ground black pepper

1 jalapeño, minced, plus more for garnish (optional)

½ cup/45 g fine saltine cracker crumbs

1 Heat a Dutch oven or cast-iron skillet over medium-high heat until hot. Add the beef and onion, breaking up the meat with a wooden spoon. Cook until the beef is well browned and the onion has softened and taken on some color. (See note on page 147 about using an aluminum slow cooker insert.)

2 Transfer the beef to the slow cooker and add the remaining ingredients.

3 Cook on high for 3 hours or on low for 6 hours. The chili is done when the beans are easily pierced with a fork. Taste and adjust the seasoning if necessary.

SUBSTITUTIONS

Ground Beef	2 pounds/910 g ground chicken (not extra-lean)	2 pounds/910 g ground pork (not extra-lean)
Red Kidney Beans	no change to recipe	2 (15.5-ounce/440 g) cans cannellini beans
Tomato Sauce	1 (28-ounce/795 g) can crushed tomatoes	no change to recipe
Saltine Crumbs	2 tablespoons cornmeal	2 tablespoons masa flour

Classic Recipe
SLOW-COOKER SLOPPY JOES

On the sloppy joe spectrum, things can go from sloppy fun to a big sloppy mess pretty quickly. To achieve that perfect equilibrium of fun enough for kids to eat without losing total structural integrity, you need to cook the meat just long enough so it is tender but not turning to mush. Also, and importantly, you need to toast the buns to create a barrier for all of that juicy meat and keep them from becoming soggy.

The filling for these sloppy joes spends all day simmering in a perfectly balanced brown sugar and garlic tomato sauce that will make your whole house smell delicious. And because it's a slow-cooker recipe, it just takes a few minutes of prep work in the morning. However, the truest testament to its deliciousness came from my youngest son, whose first word, "sloppy," was inspired by this dish.

NOTE: If you want to leave this to cook all day while you're at work, you can also cook for as long as 8 hours, just adding 1 cup/235 ml of water.

Serves 4

1½ pounds/680 g
lean ground beef

1 tablespoon
vegetable oil

½ yellow onion,
chopped

½ green bell pepper,
cored, seeded, and
chopped

1 clove garlic, minced

¾ cup/180 ml ketchup

2 teaspoons yellow
mustard

2 tablespoons light
brown sugar

½ teaspoon kosher
salt

¼ teaspoon coarsely
ground black pepper

Buns, for serving

1 Heat a large cast-iron or other heavy skillet over medium-high heat. Add the ground beef in one chunk and brown until a deep brown crust forms on the bottom, about 5 minutes. Then, break up the meat and continue cooking until it is completely cooked through, 5 to 6 minutes. Remove the beef from the pan. You can also do this in an aluminum insert. See note on page 147.

2 Add the vegetable oil to the pan, then add the onion, bell pepper, and garlic and cook for 3 to 4 minutes, stirring occasionally, until the onion is translucent.

3 Add the beef and vegetables to the slow cooker, along with the ketchup, mustard, brown sugar, salt, and pepper. Stir well. Cook on low for 4 hours.

4 *To serve:* I love serving sloppy joes on brioche buns. Spread both halves of the split buns with a smear of butter or mayonnaise and sprinkle with some shredded cheddar cheese before toasting, to create a crispy, cheesy moisture barrier between the buns and the filling.

SUBSTITUTIONS

Ground Beef	1½ pounds/680 g ground pork	1½ pounds/680 g ground chicken (not extra-lean)
Green Bell Pepper	8 ounces/225 g mushrooms, minced	1 cup/140 g minced carrots
Ketchup	½ cup/120 ml barbecue sauce plus ¼ cup/60 ml water	no change to recipe

CUBAN PORK

This recipe was made up on the spot after a bout of feverish inspiration while watching the movie *Chef*. I created a hybrid from one of my favorite recipes for carnitas and a recipe for pork roast. Don't let the jalapeños scare you off: They don't add much spice to the dish, but they do give it lots of flavor. If you would like it a bit spicier, add ¼ teaspoon red pepper flakes. We love to eat this with rice (either plain or the Easy Mexican Rice on page 79) and garlicky carrots. I also stuff leftovers into burritos or use them as a topping for nachos. And, of course, this makes a delicious Cuban sandwich. *Serves 4*

2 tablespoons vegetable oil

1 (4-pound/1.8 kg) boneless pork shoulder roast

2 teaspoons kosher salt

¼ teaspoon coarsely ground black pepper

¼ cup/60 ml orange juice (about ½ orange)

¼ cup/60 ml freshly squeezed lime juice (about 2 limes)

2 teaspoons ground cumin

2 teaspoons dried oregano

4 cloves garlic, minced

1 jalapeño, seeded and minced

1 tablespoon cornstarch, dissolved in 1 tablespoon water (optional)

Pickled red onions, cilantro, and lime for serving (optional)

1 Heat the canola oil in a large pot over medium-high heat.

2 Meanwhile, season the pork with the salt and pepper. Once the oil is hot, add the pork to the pot and brown on all sides, about 3 to 5 minutes per side. Remove from the heat.

3 Add the orange juice, lime juice, cumin, oregano, garlic, and jalapeño to a slow cooker and mix together. Add the pork and turn it in the mixture until well coated.

4 Cook on high for 6 hours or on low for 8 hours. The pork is done when it is easily pierced with a fork. Serve with pickled red onions, cilantro, and lime, if desired.

NOTE: *If you want a thicker sauce, 30 minutes before the pork is done, skim the fat off the top and stir in the cornstarch slurry. Continue to cook until the meat is done.*

SUBSTITUTIONS

Pork Shoulder	1 (4-pound/1.8 kg) pork loin roast	4 pounds/1.8 kg country-style pork ribs
Lime Juice	¼ cup/60 ml lemon juice (about 1 large lemon)	no change to recipe
Jalapeño	1 canned chipotle pepper in adobo sauce	2 bay leaves
Cornstarch	2 tablespoons all-purpose flour mixed with 2 tablespoons water	no change to recipe

BEER-AND-ONION BRISKET

The beauty of brisket is that it's just as delicious served as leftovers as it is the day it's made. Many brisket recipes call for wine, but I think beer offers a nice, slightly lighter alternative. Choose beer you love—if you like stout, use one; if you prefer a lighter pilsner style, go for it.

I serve this for dinner parties or game-day get-togethers—or any other time there's a crowd. When I have leftovers, I'll usually turn them into sandwiches: Slice the meat thin, remove any excess fat, and sear the slices in a hot skillet. Tuck the slices into toasted long rolls, spread with a thin layer of butter, and top with Swiss cheese or provolone. And if you want to take these to an entirely new level, you can dip them into some of the warmed-up leftover sauce, like a French dip. *Serves 6 to 8*

2 tablespoons vegetable oil

One (4-pound/1.8-kg) beef brisket

1 teaspoon kosher salt

½ teaspoon coarsely ground black pepper

2 yellow onions, cut into wedges

2 cups/475 ml beef broth or 2 teaspoons Better Than Bouillon beef base dissolved in 2 cups/475 ml warm water

1 (12-ounce/355 ml) can or bottle beer

8 ounces/225 g mushrooms, trimmed and halved

1 tablespoon chopped fresh thyme

3 cloves garlic, minced

1 tablespoon olive oil

1 Preheat the oven to 325°F/165°C.

2 Heat the oil in a large Dutch oven over medium-high heat. Meanwhile, season the brisket with the salt and pepper. Once the oil is hot, add the brisket and brown well on both sides, about 5 minutes per side. Remove the meat and set aside.

3 Add the onions to the pot and allow them to cook for a few minutes, getting a little color. Return the brisket to the pot, setting it on the bed of onions. Add the beef broth and beer.

4 Cover the pot, transfer to the oven, and cook for 2 hours.

5 Add the mushrooms, thyme, garlic, and olive oil to the pot and cook for another hour. The brisket should easily flake when a fork is inserted into the meat.

SUBSTITUTIONS

Brisket	1 (4-pound/1.8 kg) chuck roast	1 (5-pound/2.3 kg) boneless pork shoulder roast
Beer	1½ cups/355 ml red wine	no change to recipe
Mushrooms	3 stalks celery, cut into 2-inch/5 cm chunks	no change to recipe

JAMAICAN JERK VEGGIE BURGERS

I love veggie burgers, and I could eat them every day. I've gone through phases when I even have, which is partly why I came up with this variation—to add a little variety and keep things interesting.

As any veggie burger aficionado will tell you, texture is everything. This one gets its perfect texture from roasted sweet potatoes, which are mashed with black beans. They hold together beautifully in a burger and make for a super-satisfying, hearty main course. Jamaican jerk seasoning adds an unexpected and excitingly bright flavor. *Serves 6*

---

1 large sweet potato (to yield 2 cups chopped), peeled and cut into ½-inch/13 mm chunks

1 yellow onion, cut into ½-inch/13 mm chunks

½ teaspoon kosher salt

¼ cup/60 ml vegetable oil

2 cloves garlic, minced

1 (15-ounce/425 g) can black beans, drained and rinsed

1 large egg

1 cup/80 g panko (Japanese bread crumbs)

2 tablespoons mild jerk seasoning

Buns, lettuce, guacamole, or sliced avocado, for serving

1 Preheat the oven to 375°F/190°C.

2 Toss the sweet potato and onion with the salt and half the vegetable oil and spread out on a large sheet pan. Roast for 30 minutes, then allow to cool for about 5 minutes.

3 Add the sweet potato, onions, garlic, and black beans to a large bowl and mash them together using a potato masher. Add the egg, panko, and jerk seasoning and mix well.

4 Form the mixture into 6 patties and place them on a clean sheet pan. Brush them with the remaining oil. Bake for 25 to 30 minutes.

5 Serve the burgers on buns with lettuce and guacamole or sliced avocado.

NOTE: *Leftover burgers can be refrigerated for up to 5 days or frozen for up to 3 months; if frozen, thaw in the refrigerator before reheating. To reheat, brush with vegetable oil and heat in a toaster oven or conventional oven at 400°F/205°C for 8 to 10 minutes.*

SUBSTITUTIONS

Sweet Potato	2 cups/285 g chopped Yukon Gold potatoes (½-inch/13 mm chunks)	no change to recipe
Garlic	2 teaspoons minced ginger	no change to recipe
Canned Black Beans	1 (15-ounce/425 g) can chickpeas, drained and rinsed	2 cups/395 g cooked lentils
Panko	1 cup/100 g bread crumbs	1 cup/90 g crushed saltines
Jerk Seasoning	2 tablespoons Cajun seasoning	no change to recipe

CURRY-AND-COCONUT-RICE CASSEROLE

A classic chicken and rice casserole is a perennial favorite—easy and satisfying—and this recipe takes it down a delicious curry and coconut path. This version was born one night when I realized I had just a few tablespoons of green curry sauce left in the jar and my youngest had taken the lid off it and lost it. Hating food waste, I wanted to find a way to use it right away, and in a recipe where not much was needed. Two lessons learned: Necessity is sometimes the mother of invention and keep toddlers away from the fridge! *Serves 4 to 6*

6 bone-in, skin-on chicken thighs

1 teaspoon kosher salt

¼ teaspoon coarsely ground black pepper

2 tablespoons Thai green curry paste

1 cup/235 ml coconut milk

1 bunch green onions, chopped

2 cups/475 ml chicken broth

4 cloves garlic, minced

2 cups/370 g long-grain white rice

1 Preheat the oven to 350°F/175°C.

2 Season the chicken with the salt and pepper, then place in a 9 × 13-inch/23 × 33 cm baking dish.

3 In a medium saucepan, bring the curry paste, coconut milk, half of the green onions, and the chicken broth to a boil.

4 Add the garlic and rice to the baking dish, then pour in the broth mixture.

5 Bake, covered, for 60 minutes, or until the chicken is cooked through and the rice is fluffy.

6 Garnish with the remaining green onions.

SUBSTITUTIONS

Chicken Thighs	12 chicken drumsticks
Green Onions	2 teaspoons sesame seeds
Garlic	1 tablespoon minced ginger

BAKED SPRING MAC AND GREENS

This mac and cheese is delightfully green and springy, and it was one of the first green foods I got our kids to eat. We told them it was a Dr. Seuss recipe, and they were sold. Parenting win! Now they ask for green mac and cheese instead of the standard orange version. *Serves 4*

1 teaspoon kosher salt, plus more for the pasta cooking water

1 pound/455 g penne

4 tablespoons/55 g unsalted butter

¼ cup/30 g all-purpose flour

4 cups/950 ml whole milk

¼ teaspoon coarsely ground black pepper

2 cups/225 g shredded mozzarella cheese

1 cup/235 ml jarred pesto

2 cups/270 g frozen peas

2 cups/180 g broccoli florets

1 Preheat the oven to 350°F/175°C.

2 Bring a large pot of heavily salted water to a boil. Add the pasta and cook for 1 minute shy of the package directions; drain.

3 Add the butter and flour to a Dutch oven set over medium heat. Heat until the butter is melted and whisk well.

4 Slowly add the milk to the pot, whisking until smooth. Season with the 1 teaspoon salt and the pepper.

5 Add half the mozzarella and half the pesto and cook, stirring, until smooth. Remove from the heat.

6 Add the pasta to a large bowl, along with the peas and broccoli. Pour the sauce over and stir to coat.

7 In a 9 × 13-inch/23 × 33 cm baking dish, layer the mac and cheese beginning with half of the pasta mixture, then half of the remaining pesto, and then half of the remaining mozzarella. Repeat to make another layer.

8 Bake the mac and cheese for 20 to 25 minutes, until the top is crispy.

SUBSTITUTIONS

Penne	8 ounces/225 g lasagna sheets, cooked	no change to recipe
Peas	2 cups/310 g frozen spinach (thawed, drained, and squeezed dry)	1 pound/455 g asparagus, trimmed and cut into 2-inch/5 cm chunks
Broccoli	1 pound/455 g Brussels sprouts, shaved	2 cups/135 g thinly sliced kale

CHICKEN CAESAR PENNE

Baked pastas don't have to be all about red sauce or mac and cheese. This chicken pasta dish with homemade Caesar is like putting a cozy sweater around the famous dressing—warm and inviting—and topping it all off with a crispy Ritz cracker crust.
Serves 4

½ teaspoon kosher salt, plus more for the chicken and pasta cooking water

2 boneless, skinless chicken breasts

1 pound/455 g penne

¼ teaspoon coarsely ground black pepper

¼ cup/60 ml olive oil

¼ cup/60 ml vegetable oil

¼ cup/60 ml fresh lemon juice (from 1 large lemon)

3 cloves garlic, minced

2 teaspoons Worcestershire sauce

6 ounces/170 g Parmesan cheese, grated

4 tablespoons/55 g unsalted butter

20 Ritz crackers, crushed into fine crumbs

1 Preheat the oven to 350°F/175°C.

2 Bring a large pot of salted water to a boil. Cut the chicken into 1-inch/2.5 cm cubes and add them to the boiling water. Cook for 4 to 5 minutes and then, using a slotted spoon, remove the chicken and place in a bowl.

3 Return the water to a boil and add the pasta. Cook for 1 minute shy of the instructions on the box; drain.

4 In a medium bowl, mix together the ½ teaspoon salt, pepper, olive oil, vegetable oil, lemon juice, garlic, Worcestershire sauce, and Parmesan cheese.

5 Toss the pasta and chicken with the dressing and place in a 9 × 13-inch/23 × 33 cm baking pan.

6 In a microwave-safe bowl, melt the butter. Add the Ritz cracker crumbs, stirring until the crackers have fully absorbed the butter. Sprinkle this mixture over the pasta.

7 Bake for 20 to 25 minutes, until the topping is crispy.

SUBSTITUTIONS

Chicken	2 pounds/910 g (13–15 count) shrimp	no change to recipe	no change to recipe
Penne	4 cups/820 g cooked rice	no change to recipe	no change to recipe
Cracker Crumbs	1 cup/80 g panko (Japanese bread crumbs)	¾ cup/75 g bread crumbs	2 cups/180 g broccoli florets, stirred into the pasta

CHICKEN WITH
40 CLOVES OF GARLIC

Back in my private-cheffing days, I would routinely add this classic French dish to my proposed weekly menus for clients. Nine times out of ten, they would cross it off because they were worried about their kids hating the garlic. I got in the habit of offering it "just to try." Without fail, every family came back with raves, including from the kids, who enjoyed mopping up the sauce with bread. The cooking tames the garlic and transforms it into a mellow accent. Just be sure to have a baguette on hand for the sauce. *Serves 4*

4 skin-on, bone-in chicken thighs

½ teaspoon kosher salt

¼ teaspoon coarsely ground black pepper

⅓ cup/40 g all-purpose flour

¼ cup/60 ml olive oil

40 cloves garlic, from about 3 to 4 heads, peeled

1 cup/235 ml chicken broth

¾ cup/180 ml white wine (I use Chardonnay, but use whatever you enjoy drinking)

⅛ teaspoon grated nutmeg

1 tablespoon chopped fresh tarragon

1 Preheat the oven to 350°F/175°C.

2 Season the chicken with the salt and pepper, then dredge in the flour.

3 Heat the olive oil in a large skillet over medium-high heat. When it is hot, add the chicken skin side down and cook for 4 to 5 minutes on each side, until crispy and nicely browned. Transfer to a baking dish.

4 Reduce the heat to medium-low and add the garlic. Cook until the garlic just begins to turn brown, stirring frequently to avoid burning it, 2 to 3 minutes.

5 Add the chicken broth, white wine, and nutmeg and stir well, scraping the bottom of the pan to release any bits of chicken or garlic. Let the sauce cook for 3 to 4 minutes, until it has thickened slightly, then pour it over the chicken.

6 Bake, uncovered, until the chicken is nicely browned on top and the juices run clear when it is pricked with a knife, 25 to 30 minutes. Garnish with the tarragon before serving.

SUBSTITUTIONS

Chicken Thighs	4 bone-in pork loin chops
Tarragon	1 tablespoon chopped fresh thyme

SPANISH CHICKEN WITH OLIVES

This dish offers a quick tour through the Mediterranean: I associate the olives with Greece, but the cumin gives it a distinctly Spanish vibe. Regardless of where the ingredients come from, it's a rich and earthy comfort food with meltingly tender onions and fluffy rice flavored by chicken broth. *Serves 4*

2 tablespoons olive oil

4 bone-in, skin-on chicken thighs

1 teaspoon kosher salt

¼ teaspoon coarsely ground black pepper

1 yellow onion, diced

3 cloves garlic, minced

2 cups/475 ml chicken broth

1 teaspoon ground cumin

1 cup/185 g long-grain white rice

1 cup/155 g green olives stuffed with pimentos

1 Preheat the oven to 350°F/175°C.

2 Heat the oil in a Dutch oven or large oven-safe skillet with lid over medium-high heat. Meanwhile, season the chicken with the salt and pepper. When the oil is hot, add the chicken and cook until browned on both sides, 4 to 5 minutes per side.

3 Remove the chicken from the pan, lower the heat to medium, and add the onion and garlic. Cook until the onion is softened, 5 to 6 minutes.

4 Add the chicken broth and cumin, stir well, and bring to a boil. Add the rice and the olives and stir to combine. Return the chicken to the pan, skin side up.

5 Cover the pan, transfer to the oven, and bake for 60 minutes, until the chicken is tender and all the liquid has been absorbed.

SUBSTITUTIONS

Chicken Thighs	8 chicken drumsticks
Onion	Pinch of saffron threads

STUFFED ANTIPASTO CHICKEN

This dish looks like hasselback chicken that fell into an Italian hoagie. Our kids love it because of its fun visual presentation; we love it because it's playful and gets them outside their comfort zone. *Serves 4*

4 boneless, skinless chicken breasts

2 tablespoons vegetable oil

½ teaspoon kosher salt

¼ teaspoon coarsely ground black pepper

½ teaspoon dried oregano

½ teaspoon garlic powder

8 slices pepperoni, diced

2 slices ham, diced

2 slices provolone cheese, diced

2 pepperoncini, quartered

1 Preheat the oven to 400°F/205°C.

2 Rub the chicken with the vegetable oil and season with the salt, pepper, oregano, and garlic powder.

3 Make 5 slits in the top of each chicken breast, about 1½ inches/ 4 cm deep and 2 to 3 inches/5 to 8 cm long.

4 Mix the pepperoni, ham, provolone, and pepperoncini in a bowl. Stuff this mixture into the slits in the chicken.

5 Place the chicken on a sheet pan and bake for 28 to 30 minutes, until the edges of the deli meats are browned and crispy and the cheese is melted and browned.

SUBSTITUTIONS

Pepperoni	8 slices salami, diced	no change to recipe
Ham	½ cup/65 g diced red onion	no change to recipe
Provolone Cheese	2 ounces/57 g mozzarella cheese, diced	¼ cup/25 g grated Parmesan cheese

COCONUT CURRY CHICKEN

This is as close to "set it and forget it" as it gets. The curry is deliciously mild and the chicken is incredibly tender. If you'd like to dress it up, you can top it with chopped cashews or toasted coconut. *Serves 4*

4 bone-in, skin-on chicken thighs

1 tablespoon Thai green curry paste

1 tablespoon minced fresh ginger

2 cloves garlic, minced

¼ teaspoon kosher salt

Grated zest and juice of 1 lime (about 2 tablespoons juice)

1 (13.5-ounce/400 ml) can coconut milk

¼ cup/10 g chopped cilantro

1 Preheat the oven to 375°F/190°C.

2 Remove the skin from the chicken thighs and place the thighs in a Dutch oven.

3 In a large bowl, combine the curry paste, ginger, garlic, salt, lime zest and juice, coconut milk, and cilantro and stir well. Pour this mixture over the chicken, turning the chicken to coat.

4 Cover the pot, transfer to the oven, and bake for 35 to 40 minutes, until the thighs are cooked through and tender.

SUBSTITUTIONS

Chicken Thighs	8 chicken legs
Ginger	1 tablespoon garlic-ginger paste

Classic Recipe
MEATLOAF (WITH VARIATIONS)

This time-tested meatloaf recipe never fails me, and as a bonus, leftover slices are sturdy enough to sear in butter for killer meatloaf sandwiches. *Serves 6*

1 cup/235 ml whole milk

1 cup/100 g bread crumbs

1 large egg

½ yellow onion, diced

½ teaspoon dried thyme

½ teaspoon kosher salt

¼ teaspoon coarsely ground black pepper

1½ pounds/680 g lean (85/15) ground beef

1 tablespoon Worcestershire sauce

1 Preheat the oven to 350°F/175°C.

2 In a large bowl, stir together the milk and bread crumbs until the milk is absorbed.

3 Whisk in the egg, then stir in the onion, thyme, salt, and pepper.

4 Add the beef and mix with your hands until well combined. Transfer the mixture to a 9 × 5-inch/23 × 13 cm loaf pan.

5 Drizzle the Worcestershire sauce over the meatloaf.

6 Bake, uncovered, for 60 to 65 minutes on a rimmed baking sheet (to catch drips), until the meatloaf is browned on top and cooked through; the texture will be firm to the touch and a meat thermometer will read 155°F/70°C.

Meatloaf Variations

BBQ BACON: Add ½ minced green bell pepper to the meat mixture. Cover meatloaf with 6 bacon strips and brush with barbecue sauce.

ITALIAN PARMESAN: Add 1 teaspoon dried oregano and ¼ cup/25 g grated Parmesan cheese to the meat mixture. Glaze the meatloaf with ½ cup/120 ml marinara sauce.

GLAZED: Mix ½ cup/120 ml ketchup, 1 tablespoon yellow mustard, and 1 tablespoon light brown sugar to glaze the meatloaf.

TACO: Omit the thyme and add 2 tablespoons taco seasoning and 1 cup/115 g shredded cheddar cheese to the meat mixture. Top the meatloaf with 1 cup/235 ml enchilada sauce.

CAJUN: Heat 2 tablespoons oil in a large skillet over medium heat. Add the onion, ½ cup/50 g minced celery, and ½ cup/75 g minced green bell pepper and cook until softened. Add this to the meat mixture with 1 tablespoon Cajun seasoning.

SUBSTITUTIONS

Bread Crumbs	1¼ cups/100 g panko (Japanese bread crumbs)	1 cup/90 g crushed saltines (omit the salt)	4 slices stale white bread, crumbled
Ground Beef	1½ pounds/680 g ground chicken (not extra-lean)	1½ pounds/680 g ground turkey (not extra-lean)	no change to recipe

MUSHROOM AND WHITE WINE ORZO

This is like a faux risotto, but so much easier because it doesn't need half an hour of constant attention and stirring. Cooking orzo in broth adds tons of flavor, and every ingredient in this recipe pulls its weight. Serve it alongside a rotisserie chicken for an effortless weeknight meal. This could easily become a vegetarian main dish, especially if you kick up the number of mushrooms. Or, if you have shrimp on hand, throw in several a few minutes before the orzo is done. *Serves 4*

4 tablespoons
(½ stick)/55 g
unsalted butter

1 yellow onion, diced

1 cup/100 g orzo

8 ounces/225 g
cremini mushrooms,
sliced

3 cloves garlic, minced

1 cup/235 ml
vegetable broth

½ cup/120 ml white
wine

½ teaspoon kosher
salt

¼ teaspoon coarsely
ground black pepper

½ cup/50 g grated
Parmesan cheese

1 Melt the butter in a large pot over medium heat. Add the onion and cook, stirring occasionally, until caramelized, 8 to 10 minutes.

2 Add the orzo and mushrooms and cook until the mushrooms are browned, about 5 minutes. Add the garlic and cook for 1 minute, or until fragrant but not browned.

3 Add the vegetable broth, wine, salt, and pepper, stir, and bring to a boil.

4 Reduce the heat to low and cook for 8 minutes, or until the orzo is just tender.

5 Add the Parmesan cheese just before serving.

PEANUT SESAME NOODLES

I love this dish hot or cold—maybe even more cold. When I lived in Los Angeles, my husband and I used to take these noodles with us to the Hollywood Bowl for outdoor concerts during the summer. With or without grilled meat or some canned tuna, it makes a great picnic lunch or dinner. Looking to dress it up? Sliced bell peppers, carrots, broccoli, and zucchini are all good vegetable mix-ins, and sesame seeds or chopped green onions are great toppings. *Serves 4*

Kosher salt

1 pound/455 g thin spaghetti

2 tablespoons sesame oil

¼ cup/60 ml peanut butter

¼ cup/60 ml honey

⅓ cup/80 ml low-sodium soy sauce

¼ cup/60 ml rice vinegar

2 cloves garlic, minced

1 Bring a large pot of heavily salted water to a boil. Add the pasta and cook for 1 minute shy of the package directions.

2 Drain the pasta, reserving ½ cup/120 ml of the pasta water.

3 Return the pasta, along with the reserved cooking water, to the pot and set over medium heat.

4 Add the sesame oil, peanut butter, honey, soy sauce, rice vinegar, and garlic and toss well until the peanut butter has melted and the sauce is fully combined.

VEGGIE FRIED RICE

Unlike plain white rice, this is a very substantial—and flavorful—side for a meal. Alongside a grilled piece of meat or fish, it makes a quick, complete dinner. There are an endless number of vegetables you can add—carrots, broccoli, snow peas (it's shown here with carrots, corn, and scallions)—so follow your heart. *Serves 6*

2 tablespoons vegetable oil

1 tablespoon sesame oil

2 cups/370 g long-grain white rice

¾ cup/105 g chopped carrots

¾ cup/100 g frozen peas

¾ cup/100 g frozen corn

3 cups/710 ml chicken broth

¼ cup/60 ml low-sodium soy sauce

1 Preheat the oven to 400°F/205°C.

2 Heat the vegetable and sesame oils in a large pot over medium-high heat. Add the rice and toast for 1 minute, or until it just starts to turn translucent.

3 Remove the pot from the heat and transfer the rice to a 9 × 13-inch/23 × 33 cm baking dish.

4 Add the vegetables, broth, and soy sauce to the pot and bring to a boil.

5 Pour the liquid and vegetables over the rice, cover tightly with aluminum foil, and bake for 30 minutes.

6 Let the rice sit, covered, for 5 minutes, then fluff with a fork and serve.

GARLIC-CHEDDAR MASHED POTATOES

I promise this will be the easiest side dish on your holiday table. Baking mashed potatoes means that they don't need constant attention just before serving—they can be prepared ahead of time and reheated. They have a luscious, creamy consistency with a crispy topping, sort of like the classic French dish, Duchess potatoes, though achieved with nowhere near the amount of effort. This recipe is more of a process than hard-and-fast rules on what to include, so feel free to dress it up with additional flavorings as you desire. *Serves 8 to 10*

5 pounds/2.3 kg russet potatoes, peeled and cut into small cubes

1 teaspoon kosher salt, plus more for cooking the potatoes

8 tablespoons (1 stick)/115 g unsalted butter

8 ounces/225 g cream cheese, softened

⅓ cup/80 ml whole milk

3 cloves garlic, minced

4 ounces/115 g white cheddar cheese, shredded (about 1 cup)

1 large egg

½ teaspoon onion powder

½ teaspoon coarsely ground black pepper

1 Preheat the oven to 350°F/175°C.

2 Add the potatoes to a pot of cold salted water, bring to a boil, and cook for 7 to 10 minutes, or until they are easily pierced with a fork.

3 Drain the potatoes, return them to the pot, and mash with the butter, cream cheese, and milk.

4 Add the garlic, cheddar, egg, onion powder, 1 teaspoon salt, and the pepper to the potatoes and beat with a hand mixer until smooth.

5 Transfer the potatoes to a 9 × 13-inch/23 × 33 cm baking dish.

6 Give the potatoes another good stir to form soft peaks, then bake for 1 hour, or until they just begin to brown.

TIP: *The potatoes can be prepared up to a day in advance. Once you've added them to the baking dish, cover and refrigerate. Allow them to come to room temperature before giving them a good stir to form soft peaks, and then pop them in the oven.*

CAJUN ROASTED VEGETABLES

I try to avoid serving my vegetables with condiments like ketchup or ranch since they're loaded with sugar, salt, and calories. Roasting vegetables with a flavor-packed spice mix like Cajun seasoning makes a sauce unnecessary. And a flavorful side like this one makes dinner interesting even if you're stuck serving rotisserie chicken to a picky eater almost every night. You could turn this into a sheet-pan meal by adding some chicken thighs or sausages. Easy and delicious. *Serves 4*

2 pounds/910 g Yukon Gold potatoes, cubed

1 red bell pepper, cored, seeded, and cut into 1-inch/2.5 cm pieces

1 red onion, cut into 1-inch/2.5 cm chunks

1 pound/455 g green beans, trimmed

1 cup (145 g) fresh or frozen (135 g) sweet yellow corn kernels (from about 1 ear if using fresh)

2 cloves garlic, minced

1 tablespoon Cajun seasoning

2 tablespoons vegetable oil

1 Preheat the oven to 425°F/220°C.

2 Toss all the ingredients together in a large bowl.

3 Turn out onto a sheet pan in a single layer, making sure there is space in between the vegetables.

4 Roast for 20 minutes, then give the vegetables a stir and roast for an additional 20 minutes, or until browned and crispy.

DESSERT

3 INGREDIENTS

5 INGREDIENTS

7 INGREDIENTS

PEANUT BUTTER MUFFINS

This is one of those miracles of food science. The air incorporated while creaming the butter acts as a leavener, turning just three ingredients into muffins with a soufflé-like texture. However, the creaming step is the most important, so if you attempt to muscle though this with a whisk instead of a stand mixer, you'll end up with a dense, fudge-like consistency—and a sore arm. These muffins are naturally gluten-free, and they are delicious as dessert, but with so much protein, you can even cut back a bit on the sugar and make them for breakfast. For a fun twist, add a teaspoon of jam to the top of each one before baking. *Makes 12 muffins*

4 large eggs

¾ cup/150 g sugar

¾ cup/180 ml creamy no-stir peanut butter (not natural peanut butter)

1 Preheat the oven to 350°F/175°C. Line a muffin tin with paper liners.

2 Put the eggs in the bowl of a stand mixer fitted with the whisk attachment. Beat the eggs on high speed for 8 to 10 minutes, until they are a very pale yellow color and have become much thicker and more voluminous.

3 Add the sugar and continue to beat on high speed for another 2 to 3 minutes.

4 Add the peanut butter to a large microwave-safe bowl and microwave for 30 seconds on half power to loosen the peanut butter.

5 Add one quarter of the egg-sugar mixture to the peanut butter and fold in gently until the mixture is smooth and there are no visible streaks. Repeat with the remaining egg-sugar mixture in 3 batches.

6 Using an ice cream scoop, place ¼ cup/60 ml of batter in each muffin liner.

7 Bake for 20 to 22 minutes, until a toothpick inserted in the center of a muffin comes out clean. The muffins will be puffy when baked but deflate as they cool.

SUBSTITUTIONS

Sugar	¼ cup/50 g sugar
Peanut Butter	¾ cup/180 ml Nutella

APPLE TARTLETS

When I was a kid, one of my early cooking obsessions involved puff pastry. I loved breaking off squares of the dough and baking them—not only was it delicious, but I loved seeing it puff up in the oven. Puff pastry is very versatile, easy to handle, and all the hard work has been done for you if you buy frozen puff pastry. In my mind, it's the ultimate baking cheat. Here, just two other ingredients make a dessert that tastes exactly like apple pie. The brown sugar becomes caramelized and the apples release just enough moisture to perfume the dessert without making it soggy. *Makes 12 tartlets*

1 sheet frozen puff pastry, thawed (from a 17.3-ounce/490 g package)

3 Granny Smith apples, skin left on, cored and thinly sliced

½ cup/110 g packed light brown sugar

1 Preheat the oven to 400°F/205°C. Line a sheet pan with a silicone baking mat or grease the pan with vegetable oil.

2 Open the sheet of puff pastry and cut into 3 strips along the fold lines, then cut each strip into 4 rectangles so you have 12 pieces. Arrange on the prepared pan.

3 Arrange the apple slices in the middle of the rectangles, overlapping them. Sprinkle the brown sugar over the apples.

4 Bake the tartlets for 15 minutes, or until golden brown.

5 Let cool for 2 to 3 minutes, then serve.

SUBSTITUTIONS

Puff Pastry	1 (8-ounce/225 g) tube crescent dough	no change to recipe
Apples	24 strawberries, hulled and thinly sliced	6 pears, halved, cored, and thinly sliced
Brown Sugar	8 ounces/225 g cream cheese, softened	1 cup/235 ml Nutella

CHOCOLATE TRUFFLES

One of my favorite cooking "party tricks" involves combining heavy cream and semisweet chocolate chunks, microwaving them for a few minutes, giving the mixture a quick stir, and seeing it transform into a silky chocolate ganache. Here I take that ganache and just add a bit more chocolate to form a base for truffles. Once the mixture has cooled, you can scoop it into truffles and roll them in either powdered sugar or cocoa powder, or a mix of the two. Don't fret if your balls aren't perfectly round. It's better to roll them quickly, even if imperfectly, because your hands will heat up the chocolate and cause the truffles to melt.

A word about choosing your chocolate: Select high-quality chocolate discs or a bar; don't use chocolate chips, which are designed to keep their shape, not melt, when heated. *Makes about 30 truffles*

---

2 cups/475 ml heavy cream

1 pound 5 ounces/ 595 g semisweet chocolate discs, or bar chocolate, chopped into chunks

2 cups unsweetened cocoa powder (190 g) or powdered sugar (250 g), or a combination, for rolling

1 Add the heavy cream and chocolate to a large microwave-safe bowl and microwave on high for 3 minutes. Let sit for 3 to 4 minutes, then whisk for 3 to 4 minutes, until the mixture is smooth and shiny.

2 Place plastic wrap directly on the surface of the mixture and refrigerate for at least 4 hours, or until firm enough to mold.

3 Using a tablespoon, scoop up spoonfuls of the cold mixture and roll into 1-inch/2.5 cm balls. Roll these quickly in cocoa powder or powdered sugar (or a mix). Keep refrigerated until ready to serve.

SUBSTITUTIONS

Heavy Cream	2 cups/475 ml full-fat coconut milk	2 ripe avocados, mashed
Cocoa Powder	no change to recipe	2 cups/384 g chocolate sprinkles or grated chocolate (265 g)

BROWN SUGAR SHORTBREAD

Browning butter is an easy way to add nuanced flavor to baked goods without a lot of extra or fancy ingredients. And when you mix brown sugar into the brown butter, you get an incredibly flavorful cookie with a rich caramel-y taste—the perfect treat with coffee or tea. *Makes 24 cookies*

16 tablespoons (2 sticks)/225 g unsalted butter

2 cups/255 g all-purpose flour

½ cup/110 g packed light brown sugar

⅛ teaspoon salt

1 teaspoon vanilla extract

TIP: *Cook the butter in a pan with a light-colored bottom so you can see the color of the butter as it browns.*

1 Melt the butter in a stainless steel saucepan over medium heat, stirring constantly until it begins to foam. Keep stirring until the butter turns an amber color, 4 to 5 minutes. Immediately pour into a heatproof bowl and let cool.

2 Transfer the butter to the freezer and freeze until just solid.

3 Preheat the oven to 325°F/165°C. Line a 9 × 13-inch/23 × 33 cm baking dish with parchment paper.

4 Add the butter to the bowl of a stand mixer fitted with the paddle attachment and mix on medium speed for 30 seconds. Reduce the speed to low, add the flour, brown sugar, and salt, and mix until just combined. Mix in the vanilla.

5 Turn the dough out into the prepared pan and press it evenly over the bottom, all the way to the edges. Put the pan in the freezer to chill for 15 minutes.

6 Transfer the pan to the oven and bake for 30 minutes, or until the shortbread is just starting to turn golden brown.

7 Immediately after removing it from the oven, score the shortbread with a sharp knife to make 24 cookies.

8 Allow the shortbread to cool before slicing the cookies all the way through.

SUBSTITUTIONS

Brown Sugar	no change to recipe	½ cup/100 g granulated sugar
Vanilla Extract	1 tablespoon bourbon	½ teaspoon almond extract

NUTELLA BROWNIES

Along with just about every other person on the planet, I love Nutella. And, like just about every other person on the planet who has participated in more than a dozen bake sales, I was looking to mix up my standard brownie offering. With Nutella and just a little flour to give them structure, these bake up into rich, soft brownies. I was so inspired after making this baking discovery that I tried a version with Cookie Butter (a spread made from Speculoos cookies) that is equally delicious. That one is in the chart below, as are variations with peanut butter and almond butter. What can I say, I'm the queen of the bake sale.

Microwaving the Nutella in the jar on half power for 30 seconds makes it much easier to work with. Just make sure to completely remove the foil covering on the jar.

Makes 16 brownies

---

5 large eggs

1 (26.5-ounce/750 g) jar Nutella (2½ cups), slightly softened in the microwave

1 cup/125 g all-purpose flour

1 Preheat the oven to 350°F/175°C. Line a 9 × 13-inch/23 × 33 cm baking dish with parchment paper and spray with baking spray.

2 Add the eggs to a large bowl and whisk briefly.

3 Add the Nutella and mix until totally combined. Add the flour and mix until just incorporated; the batter should have no streaks visible.

4 Pour the batter into the baking dish and transfer to the oven. Bake for 22 to 24 minutes, until a toothpick inserted in the brownies comes out clean. Let cool completely.

SUBSTITUTIONS

Eggs	4 large super-ripe bananas	no change to recipe	no change to recipe
Nutella	1 cup/235 ml peanut butter plus ⅔ cup/135 g sugar	2½ cups/750 g Cookie Butter	2½ cups/580 ml almond butter plus ⅔ cup/135 g sugar
Flour	1 cup/95 g cocoa powder	1 cup/90 g oat flour (finely ground rolled oats)	no change to recipe

FLOURLESS CHOCOLATE CAKE WITH RASPBERRY SAUCE

Flourless chocolate cakes are festive and dramatic but save you from the standard headaches associated with cake making—worry over whether it will rise, and the uphill battle of frosting. I make this in a springform pan with a glass base, so it's pretty enough to take straight to the table, but you can do this with any springform pan. And speaking of pretty, the red raspberry sauce is striking against the dark cake, and its tartness cuts the richness of the chocolate. Seek out a high-quality chocolate, preferably 70% bittersweet. Any leftover cake keeps well in the fridge. *Makes 1 (9-inch/23 cm) cake*

---

12 ounces/340 g dark chocolate, preferably 70% bittersweet, chopped

16 tablespoons (2 sticks)/225 g unsalted butter, cut into cubes

1½ cups/300 g sugar

5 large eggs, at room temperature

2¼ cups/275 g fresh raspberries

1 Preheat the oven to 350°F/175°C. Spray a 9-inch/23 cm springform pan with baking spray, then wrap the exterior of the pan in aluminum foil to seal it; this will protect it from leakage in the water bath.

2 Place the chocolate and butter in a large microwave-safe bowl and heat on high in 30-second increments until fully melted, about 1½ minutes total, then stir well. Allow the mixture to cool.

3 In a large bowl, whisk together 1¼ cups/250 g of the sugar and the eggs until fully combined. Very slowly pour in the chocolate-butter mixture, whisking until it's a homogeneous mixture.

4 Pour the batter into the springform pan and place that in a baking dish that can accommodate it with at least 2 inches/5 cm on all sides. Add enough very hot water to the baking dish to come 1 inch/2.5 cm up the sides of the springform pan. Carefully transfer to the oven and bake for 75 minutes, or until the cake looks dry on top.

5 Meanwhile, make the raspberry sauce: Add the raspberries and the remaining ¼ cup/50 g sugar to a food processor and pulse for 30 seconds, or until smooth. Strain the sauce through a fine-mesh strainer to remove the seeds. Refrigerate until ready to serve.

6 Remove the springform pan from the water bath and allow to cool completely.

7 Once the cake is cool, release the springform ring and serve with the raspberry sauce.

SUBSTITUTIONS

Chocolate	1½ cups/355 ml peanut butter microwaved on half power for 30 seconds	no change to recipe
Butter	1 cup/235 ml coconut oil	6 pears, halved, cored, and thinly sliced
Eggs	3 large super-ripe bananas	no change to recipe
Raspberries	2¼ cups/325 g fresh strawberries	2 cups/290 g fresh blueberries

MINI FRUIT PIES

These muffin-tin fruit pies are the answer to one of my favorite questions—what's the fastest way to get more pie in my life? I use strawberries in this recipe, but you can make these with apples, cherries, peaches, or raspberries, or any combination thereof! In fact, I love making an assortment for the dessert table at family get-togethers and parties. You can even use the same bowl for this: Toss one type of fruit with some sugar and cornstarch and fill a few muffin cups, then throw in the next batch of fruit and repeat. Larger fruits should be finely chopped so they cook through. *Makes 12 mini pies*

Flour for rolling out the dough

1 (14-ounce/395 g) package piecrusts (2-count), chilled, or homemade (see page 26)

2 cups/290 g fresh strawberries

6 tablespoons/75 g sugar

3 tablespoons cornstarch

1 egg, beaten with 1 tablespoon water, for glazing

⅓ cup/63 g coarse sanding sugar for sprinkling (optional)

1 Preheat the oven to 350°F/175°C. Have a nonstick muffin tin ready.

2 On a floured surface, roll one sheet of pie dough to a ¼-inch/ 6 mm thickness. Using a 3½-inch/9 cm round cookie cutter, cut out 12 circles. Place a circle of dough into each muffin cup, ensuring that it is centered. Then, adding more flour to your work surface as needed, roll out the second sheet of pie dough to a ¼-inch/6 mm thickness. Using a 2-inch/5 cm round cookie cutter, cut out 12 circles.

3 Lightly toss the strawberries, sugar, and cornstarch together in a large bowl. Spoon a few tablespoons of the filling into each muffin cup.

4 Top each mini pie with a 2-inch/5 cm circle of dough. Brush lightly with the egg wash and then add a sprinkling of the coarse sanding sugar, if using. Place the muffin tin in the freezer for 10 minutes.

5 Transfer the pan to the oven and bake for 20 to 25 minutes, until the tops of the pies are golden brown and the fruit is bubbling when poked with knife. Let cool completely before serving.

SUBSTITUTIONS

Strawberries	2 cups/310 g pitted cherries	2 cups/310 g chopped peaches	2 cups/290 g fresh blueberries

S'MORES CUPS

This dessert is the result of about a decade of tinkering with the campfire classic, which, not to make waves, could use a few improvements. I started by making this as a big s'mores bar, where the graham cracker crust was literally 2 inches/5 cm thick. It was quite possibly the most delicious thing on the face of the earth, but not only was it hard to justify the amount of butter needed to hold it together, it was nearly impossible to slice without crumbling.

These cups proved to be the answer. They have enough graham cracker goodness to satisfy but contain a saner amount of butter, and they are easy to make and to serve.

Makes 12 s'mores cups

---

18 graham crackers (2 packs), crushed into fine crumbs

8 tablespoons (1 stick)/115 g unsalted butter, melted

1 tablespoon sugar

½ cup/120 ml heavy cream

1⅓ cups (8 ounces)/ 225 g milk chocolate discs

4 cups/172 g mini marshmallows

⅛ teaspoon salt

1 In a large bowl, combine the graham cracker crumbs, butter, and sugar and stir until the mixture resembles wet sand. Using a spoon, divide this mixture equally among the 12 cups of a muffin tin and then press evenly over the bottoms and sides, using the back of the spoon or your fingertips.

2 Add the heavy cream and chocolate to a microwave-safe bowl and heat on high for 1 minute, or until the chocolate is completely melted. Give it a good stir. Let cool for a few minutes, then spoon into the graham cracker cups. Top with the marshmallows.

3 Turn on the broiler. Place the muffin tin on the top rack under the broiler for 30 seconds, or until the marshmallows are browned and melted.

4 Transfer the muffin tin to the refrigerator and allow the s'mores to harden, about 30 minutes.

5 To serve, use a thin knife to gently pry the cups out of the tin.

SUBSTITUTIONS

Heavy Cream	½ cup/65 g powdered sugar
Chocolate Chips	¾ cup/180 ml Nutella

Candy Bar Cheat Sheet

ALMOND JOY: ½ cup (80 g) chocolate chips, ¼ cup (40 g) chopped almonds, ½ cup (50 g) toasted coconut on top

SNICKERS: 15 Rolo candies, ½ cup (125 g) chopped peanuts

ROCKY ROAD: ¼ cup (40 g) chocolate chips, ¼ cup (40 g) chopped almonds, 1 cup (50 g) mini marshmallows

TWIX: 15 Rolo candies halved, ¼ cup (40 g) chocolate chips, ¼ cup (40 g) shortbread cookie chunks

YORK PEPPERMINT PATTIES: ¼ cup (68 g) chopped York peppermint patties, ¼ cup (40 g) milk chocolate chips

100 GRAND: 15 Rolo candies, ¼ cup (40 g) chocolate chips, 1 cup (28 g) Rice Krispies cereal

REESE'S CUP: ¼ cup (40 g) chocolate chips, ¼ cup (40 g) peanut butter chips

BACK-POCKET CHOCOLATE BROWNIES

This is my basic recipe for brownies, to which I add any number of mix-ins, nuts, swirls, frostings, etc. It's delicious as is, but also not too sweet if you do opt for those extras. I feel strongly that there is a right texture for brownies, and these are more cakey than fudgey, and with just the right amount of chew. However, if you are ready to get a little crazy, boy do I have some exciting options for you. I love playing around with recipes, and trying to re-create popular candy bars is one of my favorite hobbies. Opposite you'll find my candy bar cheat sheet. Adding any one of these to the base recipe will yield a brownie like you've never had. *Makes 12 brownies*

8 tablespoons (1 stick)/115 g unsalted butter, melted and still warm, plus more for greasing the pan

⅔ cup/65 g unsweetened cocoa powder, plus more for dusting the pan

1 cup/200 g sugar

2 large eggs

¾ cup/95 g all-purpose flour

½ teaspoon baking soda

1 teaspoon salt

1 Preheat the oven to 350°F/175°C.

2 Grease the bottom and sides of an 8 × 8-inch/20 × 20 cm square baking pan with butter. Then dust with cocoa powder, tapping out the excess.

3 In a large bowl, combine the just-melted butter and the sugar. Whisk well for a minute or so, until the sugar has dissolved and the mixture has cooled.

4 Add the eggs and whisk until well combined.

5 Sift together the flour, ⅔ cup (65 g) cocoa powder, baking soda, and salt, then add to the wet ingredients in several batches, whisking until just combined. (If using mix-ins, add them here and stir just to incorporate.) Pour into the prepared baking pan.

6 Bake the brownies for 20 to 22 minutes, just until a toothpick inserted in the center comes out clean; be careful not to overbake. Let cool completely.

SUBSTITUTIONS

Eggs   1 large super-ripe banana

WHITE CHOCOLATE-RASPBERRY MOUSSE

I love serving mousse as a satisfying but not heavy finish to a meal, and I also love showcasing how varied mousse can be. For instance, this one is about the polar opposite of the Bourbon Chocolate Mousse (page 208). Whereas that one is dark, rich, and earthy, this one is bright, fresh, and citrusy. The raspberries and lemon zest make an easy sauce, which can be cooked or simply pureed. When shopping for white chocolate, seek out high-quality discs or bars. White chocolate chips are notorious for burning. *Serves 4*

1½ cups/355 ml
heavy cream

12 ounces/340 g
white chocolate
discs or bars, finely
chopped

¾ cup/90 g fresh
raspberries

½ cup/65 g
powdered sugar

Grated zest of 1 lemon

1 Add ¾ cup/180 ml of the cream to a medium saucepan and heat over medium heat until hot and slightly bubbly around the edges; don't let it come to a boil.

2 Take the cream off the heat and add the white chocolate. Stir until the chocolate is melted and completely incorporated. Set aside to cool to room temperature.

3 Add the remaining ¾ cup/180 ml cream to the bowl of a stand mixer fitted with the whisk attachment and beat on high until soft peaks form. Replace the whisk attachment with the paddle and gently mix in the cooled chocolate. Transfer to 4 bowls and chill for at least 2 hours before serving.

4 Meanwhile, make the raspberry sauce: Add the raspberries, powdered sugar, and lemon zest to a food processor and pulse for 30 seconds, or until smooth. Strain the sauce through a fine-mesh strainer to remove the seeds. Refrigerate until ready to serve.

SUBSTITUTIONS

| Raspberries | ¾ cup/125 g sliced fresh strawberries |

BOURBON CHOCOLATE MOUSSE

This is a rich and sophisticated dessert, but the level of booziness depends on you; the amount called for here adds just a whiff of bourbon, but feel free to use more to carry a bigger kick. I serve this topped with cream whipped into soft peaks, a side of cookies, and sometimes, if I'm feeling fancy, chocolate shavings. It makes a delicious pie when poured into a pre-baked shell. *Serves 4*

1 cup/235 ml heavy cream

1½ cups/255 g chopped 70% bittersweet or 60% semisweet chocolate

⅓ cup/40 g powdered sugar

3 tablespoons bourbon, or more to taste

8 large egg whites

Flaky sea salt for finishing

1 Add the heavy cream, chocolate, and powdered sugar to a large microwave-safe bowl and heat on high for 90 seconds.

2 Remove from the microwave and let sit for 3 minutes, then whisk until smooth.

3 Add the bourbon and whisk until smooth.

4 In the bowl of a stand mixer fitted with the whisk attachment, beat the egg whites on high speed until they form stiff peaks, 3 to 4 minutes.

5 Add one quarter of the egg whites to the chocolate mixture and fold in gently until incorporated. Repeat with another one quarter of the egg whites, then add the remaining egg whites and again fold in until no streaks are visible.

6 Spoon the mousse into 4 bowls and refrigerate for at least 2 hours. Sprinkle with flaky salt just before serving.

SUBSTITUTIONS

Bourbon	1 cup/43 g mini marshmallows, spread over the top of the mousse at the end, plus 2 graham crackers, crumbled on top of the marshmallows	1 tablespoon instant coffee powder

NUTELLA-MOUSSE TART

This is a show-stopping dessert and one that I love pulling out for dinner parties. The buttery, flaky crust adds some delicious crunch to the smooth hazelnut flavor of the filling. I often add a splash of Frangelico, a hazelnut liqueur, to the filling, but I don't call for it here because I hate making people feel like they need to shell out a lot of money for a bottle of alcohol when only a teaspoon or two is needed. If you have it on hand, add it; if you don't, the cake will still be spectacular. *Makes 1 (9-inch/23 cm) tart*

FOR THE CRUST

8 tablespoons (1 stick)/115 g unsalted butter, softened

¼ cup/50 g sugar

1 large egg, at room temperature

1½ cups/190 g all-purpose flour

3 tablespoons cocoa powder

¼ teaspoon salt

FOR THE MOUSSE

1 (¼-ounce/7 g) packet (2¼ teaspoons) plain gelatin powder

1 cup/235 ml Nutella

3 tablespoons unsweetened cocoa powder

1½ cups/355 ml heavy cream

1 Preheat the oven to 350°F/175°C. Line the bottom of a 9-inch/23 cm springform pan with parchment paper. Cut additional strips of parchment to line the sides of the pan.

2 Make the crust: Add the butter and sugar to a stand mixer fitted with the paddle attachment and mix on medium speed until light and fluffy, about 1 minute. Add the egg and mix until creamy. Sift together the flour, cocoa powder, and salt, then add to the stand mixer set on the lowest speed setting and mix until just combined.

3 Press the mixture evenly into the springform pan using your fingers or the back of a spoon. Bake for 20 to 25 minutes. Remove the pan from the oven and let the crust cool completely.

4 Meanwhile, make the mousse: Add the gelatin and ¼ cup/60 ml water to a saucepan and let sit for 2 to 3 minutes to soften before warming over medium-low heat for 2 to 3 minutes, until the gelatin is completely melted and no longer visible.

5 Turn off the heat and add the nutella and cocoa powder to the saucepan and whisk until smooth. Allow to cool for 10 minutes.

6 Add the 1½ cups/355 ml heavy cream to the cleaned bowl of the stand mixer fitted with the whisk attachment and whip the cream on medium-high until soft peaks form, about 1 minute.

7 Fold one third of the whipped cream into the Nutella mixture until completely combined. Fold in the remaining whipped cream just until no streaks remain. Pour the mousse into the crust and refrigerate for 3 hours.

Recipe continues on page 211

1 cup/235 ml Nutella

½ cup/120 ml
heavy cream

Chopped hazelnuts,
for garnish (optional)

8 When ready to serve: Add the Nutella and ½ cup/120 ml heavy cream to a microwave-safe bowl, cover with a wet paper towel, and microwave on half power for 1 minute. Whisk until smooth, then let cool for 5 minutes.

9 Gently spread the topping over the mousse before serving. Sprinkle with the chopped hazelnuts, if using.

SUBSTITUTIONS

| Nutella (topping) | 6 ounces/170 g bittersweet chocolate, finely chopped | 6 ounces/170 g Speculoos Cookie Butter |

BLUEBERRY COBBLER

A cobbler is an easy, no-fuss dessert that takes full advantage of bountiful seasonal fruit. And by nature of the fact that it's supposed to look rustic, it's a very forgiving dessert to make. I love getting my kids involved in making the dough. I give them ice cream scoops or big spoons and tell them the the mounds of dough should look like continents on an ocean of fruit. Once you give that an egg wash and a dusting of sugar, there's no way it won't look beautiful. Any stone fruit or berries will work here. Because this makes a big cobbler, plan on bringing it to a potluck or picnic, since there will be lots to share. *Serves 8*

FOR THE FRUIT FILLING

4 cups/580 g fresh blueberries

¼ cup/50 g sugar

2 tablespoons all-purpose flour

1 tablespoon lemon juice

FOR THE DOUGH

1 cup/125 g all-purpose flour

¼ cup/50 g sugar

1 tablespoon baking powder

¼ teaspoon salt

½ teaspoon ground cinnamon

½ cup/120 ml whole milk

6 tablespoons/85 g unsalted butter, melted, plus 1 tablespoon melted butter for glazing

1 tablespoon coarse sanding sugar (optional)

1 Preheat the oven to 375°F/190°C. Butter a 9 × 13-inch/23 × 33 cm baking dish.

2 Make the filling: Toss the blueberries with the sugar, flour, and lemon juice. Pour into the prepared baking dish and bake for 25 to 28 minutes, until the fruit is bubbling.

3 Meanwhile, make the dough: Sift together the flour, sugar, baking powder, salt, and cinnamon into a medium bowl. Whisk in the milk and the 6 tablespoons/85 g melted butter; the dough will be slightly sticky.

4 Remove the baking dish from the oven and increase the oven temperature to 400°F/205°C.

5 Scoop spoonfuls of dough over the fruit (carefully, since the dish is very hot), making sure to leave some spaces where the blueberries show through.

6 Brush the remaining 1 tablespoon melted butter over the dough and sprinkle with the coarse sugar.

7 Bake for 13 to 15 minutes, until the topping is golden brown. Let cool completely.

SUBSTITUTIONS

Blueberries	4 cups/620 g thinly sliced peaches	4 cups/435 g peeled and sliced apples
Sugar	¼ cup/55 g packed light brown sugar	no change to recipe
Cinnamon	½ teaspoon almond extract	no change to recipe

STRAWBERRY SHORTBREAD BARS

These are somewhere between a coffee cake and a strawberry shortcake—so, basically, totally amazing. *Makes 16 bars*

FOR THE DOUGH

10⅔ tablespoons/ 150 g unsalted butter, frozen and cut into small cubes

⅔ cup/145 g packed light brown sugar

1 teaspoon baking powder

¼ teaspoon salt

2 cups/255 g all-purpose flour

1 large egg

FOR THE FILLING

2 pounds/910 g fresh strawberries, hulled and cut into small chunks

2 tablespoons flour

2 tablespoons sugar

Grated zest of 1 lemon

FOR THE CRUMBLE TOPPING

8 tablespoons (1 stick)/ 115 g unsalted butter, melted

1½ cups/190 g all-purpose flour

⅔ cup/145 g packed light brown sugar

¼ cup/50 g sugar

1 Preheat the oven to 300°F/150°C. Line a 9 × 13-inch/23 × 33 cm baking pan with parchment paper.

2 Make the dough: Add the butter, brown sugar, baking powder, salt, and flour to a food processor fitted with the metal blade and pulse until crumbles form. Add the egg and pulse until just combined.

3 Turn the dough out into the prepared baking pan and press evenly into the pan. Bake for 20 minutes to firm up the crust slightly. Remove from the oven and let cool.

4 Raise the oven temperature to 350°F/175°C.

5 Make the filling: Toss the strawberries with the flour, sugar, and lemon zest. Pour onto the cooled crust.

6 Make the topping: In a medium bowl, mix the melted butter with the flour and both sugars with your hands and form into a dense ball. Then crumble the topping over the strawberries.

7 Bake the bars for 30 to 35 minutes, until the crumble topping is starting to brown and the filling is bubbly.

8 Let cool before slicing into bars.

SUBSTITUTIONS

Egg	no change to recipe	no change to recipe	no change to recipe	omit 2 tablespoons in filling
Strawberries	4 cups/ 410 g cherries, pitted	4 cups/ 580 g fresh blueberries	4 cups/ 490 g fresh raspberries	1½ cups/ 355 ml strawberry or raspberry jam
Lemon Zest	½ teaspoon almond extract	2 teaspoons vanilla extract	6 ounces/ 170 g white chocolate, melted and drizzled on top of the cooled bars	no change to recipe
Flour (filling)	no change to recipe	no change to recipe	no change to recipe	omit

CHERRY-CHEESECAKE TOASTER PASTRIES

What can I say—dessert should be fun and these are just plain, unabashed fun. I've made these for my kids' birthday parties and then brought out any sprinkles, icing, frosting, etc., I have on hand and let them decorate to their hearts' content. *Makes 8 pastries*

1 (14.1-ounce/399 g) package piecrusts (2-count), chilled, or homemade (see page 26)

Flour for rolling out the dough

½ cup/120 ml cherry preserves

4 ounces/115 g cream cheese, softened

½ cup/65 g powdered sugar

2 tablespoons whole milk

1 teaspoon vanilla extract

FOR THE GLAZE
1 egg, beaten with 1 tablespoon water

¼ cup/50 g coarse sanding sugar (optional)

1 Preheat the oven to 425°F/220°C. Line a sheet pan with parchment paper.

2 Roll out each piece of dough on a floured surface and cut each sheet into 8 rectangles, 3 × 4 inches/8 × 10 cm each.

3 Spread 1 tablespoon of cherry preserves on each of the 8 rectangles.

4 In a large bowl, whisk together the cream cheese, powdered sugar, milk, and vanilla extract.

5 Spread 1 tablespoon of the cream cheese mixture over the preserves on each rectangle.

6 Place the remaining rectangles over the rectangles with preserves and cream cheese and press the edges together with the tines of a fork to seal. Using a spatula, lift the tarts onto the lined sheet pan. Glaze each with egg wash and a sprinkling of the sanding sugar, if using.

7 Bake for 8 to 10 minutes, or until lightly browned. Let cool.

SUBSTITUTIONS

Piecrust	1 box (2 sheets) puff pastry (bake at 400°F/205°C for 20 to 25 minutes until golden brown)	2 (8-ounce/226 g) tubes crescent dough (bake at 375°F/190°C, for 10 to 12 minutes)
Cherry preserves	½ cup/120 ml raspberry jam	½ cup/120 ml strawberry jam
Cream Cheese	½ cup/120 ml Nutella	no change to recipe

ACKNOWLEDGMENTS

When you've grown up to be a serious adult, it's easy to forget the dreams you had as a kid. This cookbook is the fulfillment of a dream that I've had since I was little watching Martin Yan and Wolfgang Puck with sheer amazement. Seeing them weave ingredients together and bring joy to people with their recipes inspired me to want to do the same for my family. I usually only accomplished making a huge mess in the kitchen, but there were magical moments of homemade lasagna with fresh pasta and a positively delicious microwave coffee cake that I still remember so clearly. Cooking for people in my life has always brought me joy and has been my way of sharing my love for those I care about.

To the readers of my blog, you have watched the website grow from an idea that was kicked around for a few years into a life-changing experience that has allowed me to leave behind being a professional chef, stay home with my family, and watch my children grow. The blessing that this site has been to our family is immeasurable and I thank each and every one of you for the support over the years.

To my husband, you're the rock of our family and our biggest cheerleader even in your most tired moments. The website, and therefore this cookbook, simply never would have existed without your never-ending support, from working through nights after work and cooking with me during the weekends. There aren't enough words to say

thank you for who you are—for me, and for our kids. I'm the luckiest for having you in my life.

To our kids, you've mastered staying out of ingredients and dishes that are "for mommy's work" until you get the all-clear. I love your honest reactions to foods you love (and hate) and the sheer joy you bring to our lives. Being home with you during the day, when you get home from school, and all the extra moments I feel I get with you all makes me the happiest person in the world.

To Michele and Henry, you've been the most amazing support system for our family. The running joke for anyone who knows of you is that they want to be adopted by you both. I'm so lucky to have you in our lives—your positivity and reassurance over the years has given me the confidence to leap, knowing you are there if I fall. Thank you from the bottom of my heart. Every time you've said, "Don't worry, go for it. We're here for you no matter what happens," has given us wings.

To Birdie and Pops, your support from the beginning of this endeavor was a tremendous boost to our spirits. Your words of encouragement did wonders for our confidence during times when signs of encouragement were few and far between. Even years before the blog started, I asked if you'd ever want a book of my recipes and I still remember your response: "Of course, Sweetie!" Well, it took a while, but I hope you enjoy having this book on your shelf.

To Mary Louise, you are such a loving and calming influence in my life. It can sometimes be hard to see through the weeds when I feel stuck, and you're always so willing to bring clarity and peace into my hectic life. Thank you for always being so happy to tell people about the site and the book!

To my friends, who are family in my eyes. You know I am uncomfortable being the center of attention and you've taken it upon yourselves to be the bullhorn for *Dinner Then Dessert* over the years. You've supported me and given me the pep talks I've needed in the most anxious of times, and it means everything to me.

To Jen, Janna, Sara, Hanna, Jacqui, Justin, Lewis, Duane, Teisha, Caitlin, Annabel, Alicia, and the rest of the people who have helped us on the website over the years, I would never have had the energy to keep the pace, the recipe testing, the cleaning, the cooking, the proofreading without you all.

To Sharon Bowers, my agent, you have been an amazing advocate and partner through this process. This book would not have happened but for your tenacity and advocacy on my behalf, and for your endless patience with all my emails. I appreciate you so much. Also, a huge thank you for bringing Jenny to this book.

To Jenny Wapner, you are remarkable. Working with you to write this book has been an absolute joy. You have the most remarkable way to take ten tidbits of information and make them magical and funny and witty. I wish I could have you with me every day on DTD.

To Colin Price, thank you for bringing these recipes to life with your beautiful photography. Working with you on this book was an absolute joy that I'm sorry had to end!

To Harper Design and HarperCollins, thank you for believing in *Dinner Then Dessert* and in this book. It is a dream come true and you've been kind and understanding and patient with me as we've navigated these uncharted waters over the last two years together. Thank you, especially, to Tricia Levi; you are wonderful and kind and always willing to discuss even the smallest idea or question.

INDEX

About the Author

Sabrina Snyder is a trained chef from California and the founder of the easy family-friendly recipes website DinnerthenDessert.com, which receives millions of visitors each month. She's been featured in Buzzfeed, *Cosmopolitan*, *Parade*, Yahoo, MSN, and more.